10.00

D0948666

THE HALF-GALLON QUARTER-ACRE
PAVLOVA PARADISE

Austin Mitchell

THE HALF-GALLON QUARTER-ACRE PAVLOVA PARADISE

An introduction to the wonderful people, the fulfilling life style and the fascinating spectacles which will greet the interested British immigrant on his arrival in New Zealand, a land believed by many to be the fairest jewel in the British Crown; the whole being communicated in the form of twelve letters to a new settler.

Illustrated by LES GIBBARD

WHITCOMBE AND TOMBS LIMITED

FIRST PUBLISHED JULY 1972

REPRINTED SEPTEMBER 1972

ISBN 0 7233 0349 5

Printed and published by
WHITCOMBE AND TOMBS LIMITED
P.O. Box 1465, Christchurch
AUCKLAND HAMILTON ROTORUA HASTINGS WELLINGTON
LOWER HUTT NELSON TIMARU DUNEDIN INVERCARGILL
LONDON SYDNEY MELBOURNE PERTH

Publisher's Note

When Austin Mitchell was about to leave New Zealand to return to Oxford University in 1967 we asked him to write a humorous book on this country. We had in mind something light and bright, something that would amuse and gently shake many New Zealanders' smug attitude to their homeland.

But, back in England, he decided he wanted to write a further book on the New Zealand political scene to complement a work of his we had already published—*Government by Party*. He duly wrote *Politics and People in New Zealand* and then, under persistent prompting, he produced *The Half-gallon Quarter-acre Pavlova Paradise*.

We should have known better what to expect. It is certainly humorous, but as for a gentle tilt at our way of life—well, that's not the Mitchell way. In his free-wheeling style he makes fun of most aspects of New Zealand life—even revered institutions such as the Plunket Society don't escape the Mitchell barbs. His criticism can be kindly, but it is often merciless.

Though Austin Mitchell has been away from New Zealand since 1967, he has kept himself well informed on our affairs and the book is topical. A political event that he wanted to comment on—the change in leadership of the National Party —came too late in the book's production.

Austin Mitchell is a political scientist turned television personality (he called himself a 'teledon') and he was described aptly in a review of one of his political books by John Pettigrew: 'Austin Mitchell is a professional political scientist and controversialist . . . and the combination makes for stimulating reading.'

Of *The Half-gallon Quarter-acre Pavlova Paradise,* Austin Mitchell says: 'The tone is essentially humorous, though I hope the kernels of truth are there . . . Though the traits are over-extended they represent real characteristics.' Despite his shafts he is well disposed towards us and, in the last sentence of the book, he says: 'In this nasty, overcrowded and polluted world New Zealand is as near to a people's paradise as fallible humanity is likely to get.'

Contents

WELCOME

Dear Keith,

Good luck in God's Own Country. He probably wasn't able to welcome you in person. The Wellington Airport Authority was no doubt a satisfactory stand-in. If he had been there, he'd say the same as I do: you're a lucky man.

It's a wonderful country. Not quite paradise—the National Party hasn't been in that long—but probably the best country in the world. Certainly the best in the Southern Hemisphere. Having made this deference to New Zealand sales, I must in all honesty warn you. It's a funny country. The natives have their own tribal customs and ceremonies. They also have their own susceptibilities. If an Englishman like yourself didn't find them different to the folks back home in all sorts of endearing little ways the natives couldn't bear it. Different means better. Let your indulgent smile turn into a laugh—once imply that certain things are better handled in Britain and you'll get the ritual excommunication: 'If you don't like it why don't you go home?' Ignorance of the lore is no excuse.

As a country New Zealand has one major preoccupation: New Zealand. The rest of the world ignores it, so it compensates by more and more frantic navel exercises of national belly-button studying. Later you'll be able to exploit this endearing insecurity for gain, like the other Englishmen there. At the moment you might not know how to handle it. You'll have met the first manifestation of obsession already, having been asked a thousand times how you like the country; two thousand times if you've already left the airport tarmac. This is not designed to elicit information. It is a request for reassurance, encouragement, admiration and all the other things assisted immigrants are brought in to provide.

Above all don't try to be funny: a psychiatrist might as well heap filthy jokes on patients anxious about impotence. An illustration. When I arrived in New Zealand, the first words of my kindly boss were a warning not to be critical when asked how I liked New Zealand (henceforth referred to as question number one). A reporter arrived for the routine interview with all new university staff (this being Otago, where there is little else to fill the papers). I, being young and anxious to build a reputation as the David Frost of Academe, answered question number one by saying that the lavatorial graffiti were at least more literate than in Britain (although cruder). The only thing wrong with New Zealand, I added, was the number of people asking how I liked New Zealand. There duly appeared a photograph of a leering sex maniac almost certainly arrived in Dunedin to form the Otago branch of White Slavers' International. This headed an article which hinted in scarcely veiled fashion that I had come to New Zealand because of my inability to get a job in Britain. This was, of course, true of all university staff arrivals. It had never before been made explicit, for this was before Mr Muldoon.

You must make the proper replies. An American matron might get away with saying 'it's cute'. An Englishman's response is, 'It's a great improvement on where I've just come from.' This will be either Fiji or Australia, but no one will realise. You could also try, 'Well, it's a great place to bring up children.' This does not commit *you* to any view and has

the added advantage of hinting that you will take early steps to make yourself normal (that's to say as miserable as the rest) by producing progeny. If you're still single and the predatory New Zealand girls returning home on your plane have not managed to get their claws into you, then this answer gives a subtle indication that you are suitably ashamed of your unnatural single status and are on the look-out for a decent New Zealand girl (i.e. any).

You walk a delicate tightrope, avoiding culture shock without frightening the natives. There is no one to advise you. The great sociological-anthropological machine of the American universities hasn't yet processed New Zealand, boiling it all down to a book full of tables, every generalisation significant statistically. Nor have the experts who package a country and distil its essence into a few hundred pages, or even a generalisation, plasticised New Zealand. John Gunther didn't add New Zealand to his volumes on the U.S.A., U.S.S.R. and the other major powers, and his successor went home after two days. Margaret Mead never lived with the natives in their tin-roofed huts. Raymond Postgate never sampled the Rose Cafe on Lambton Quay, to confer three stars on its Egg on Toast and none on its Egon Ronay. The authors of *See the World on Five Dollars a Day* managed only a quarter of an hour in New Zealand after the last General Wage Order. Googie Withers went back to Australia after a week's visit, complaining that she had no idea what New Zealand was like. It had been shut.

Foreigners are too taciturn, the natives too verbose. They have their gurus, though they can only afford one in each field. You could always consult Don Clarke on aesthetics, Ralph Love on poetry, Tom Skinner on etiquette or Charles Brasch on rugby. This would take too long, and pontificating for the N.Z.B.C. makes heavy demands on their time.

Similarly you would never be able to wade through the books about New Zealand. Production of books about the country is the major local industry, after plastic tikis. Books about New Zealand In Colour provided the original impetus for the Japanese economic miracle. New Zealand presses pour out books on New Zealand, if they aren't lucky enough to get the Labour Party raffle ticket account. To mention New Zealand in a book title is a guarantee of massive sales.

The main purpose of all these books is therapeutic, not diagnostic. They are the literary branch of the vast local reassurance industry. They portray New Zealand as the best place in the world, its people as the greatest blokes. Every characteristic from boozing to boorishness has to be catalogued as both endearing and admirable. Look at the abridged version of the *New Zealand Encyclopaedia*, also known as *From N to Z*, and you'll see what I mean. It bears as little relation to life in New Zealand as that section of the London telephone directory masquerading under the same title, though it's not quite as funny.

If New Zealand were as the New Zealanders see it, it would be a tourist Mecca. Every international airport from Auckland to Wanganui would throng with jumbo jets coming on trunk routes to bring American tourists to view the native customs. The Hopé Indians can stage their ghost dance at the drop of a traveller's cheque. New Zealand should restore its sacred customs for the same consideration. The mystic invocations at the rugby club 'down-trow' would be almost drowned by the whirr of movie cameras. The rich linguistic legacy of the election rituals would draw thousands. Coaches would tour vivid re-enactments of the six o'clock swill, staged by

Richard Campion and choreographed after extensive interviews with survivors. Portrayals of native courting habits in
the back of reconstructed heaps in the dunes would be an
attraction. All a dream. The tourists are a trickle not a flood.

New Zealand is not so much a country, more a way of life.
It's up to me to instruct you in the faith you're about to be
received into. Since you can't have the benefit of growing up
in it, learn it by heart. Kiwi in seven days if you memorise the
handy phrases and do the exercises. It would be a mistake to
acclimatise more quickly. Immigrants are expected to be 'different' (literally translated 'peculiar'), to smell slightly and
have insanitary habits. If they don't, then the natives might
get disorientated, begin to doubt their own superiority and
feel there's nothing left to live for. So make all sorts of little
endearing mistakes. When going to social functions make your

wife take a plate. Every immigrant will assure you that his wife did this in response to the 'ladies a plate' instruction, though readers of *Groupie* might think the injunction scandalous. Talk as if hogget was a pig or an English sociologist. No one will notice the difference. Eat your fish and chips with the paper open right out instead of tearing off the corner like the natives do. This custom is more than an admission that the fish are so pathetically small that it's the only way to keep them warm; it is also a badge of national identity. Deliberate minor mistakes will give you something to talk about in later years and keep the New Zealanders happy. Yet don't keep up the pretence too long. You have to conform and soon. Read on quickly. The period of grace won't last long.

DRAMATIS PERSONAE:
A Cast of Three Million

IF THE KIWI has one fault it's modesty. He never blows his own trumpet. It will take a couple of minutes and at least half a dozen beers before you get him to admit that New Zealand is the most honest, decent, intelligent and cleanest of nations. Almost too good for this world, which may be why New Zealanders live so far away from it. Like Clark Kent they efface themselves until wrongs are to be righted. Then with the magic cry of 'Conscription' they change into the khaki insignia of Super Kiwi, set the world to rights and come back to their island fastness. An unsuspecting world is left thinking Monty won North Africa and Lieutenant Calley made Vietnam safe for democracy. The Kiwi owns up only to Crete and Gallipoli, to save others from embarrassment.

New Zealanders are not perfect, theirs is a young country. The Ancient Greeks had a head start but the gap is being narrowed every day. If Kiwis stop to wonder why Divine Providence which treated the rest of the world so ill did so well by them, they would probably put it down to national eugenics, breeding from a good stock carefully shielded from any base or coloured genes, even blue ones. Truth is more

17

prosaic. New Zealand is what it is because it has been conditioned by isolation, by the need to make the best of what it has not got, and by smallness. And the greatest of these is smallness.

The population is maintained at a rough balance of one man equivalent to twenty-three ewe equivalents, or people to sheep—but then what's in a name, as Engelbert Humperdinck would say. This balance makes the humans better off, with the average bloke earning $2,235 at the 1966 census, the average sheep only $6. Unfortunately it upsets a combined chorus of politicians and sex maniacs who want the people to catch up on the sheep by populating or perishing, conveniently forgetting that the strain of reaching the first ten million could produce both eventualities. Yet a population of only three million, scattered over 104,000 square miles, is responsible for most of the national characteristics. God who made them tiny, make them tinier yet.

Small population means an intimate society. You'll soon begin to think that all New Zealanders know each other or even that they are all interrelated, thanks to some mysterious process of national incest. No one can arrive in a town where he doesn't have a relative, a friend, or at worst a common acquaintance of his maiden aunt's. As soon as the weather is out of the way conversations have limitless, or rather three million, prospects for mutual name swapping. The only way *you* can join in is by memorising a phone book.

A small country is unspecialised. Skills only become complex and compartmentalised in larger countries. British workmen arriving there are baffled to find that they can't just exercise their traditional skill of screwing on the doorbell— they have to help build the house as well. A uniquely irrelevant British education system trained me to know everything about one British political party from 1815 to 1830, and nothing about anything else. I arrived in New Zealand to find myself lecturing on the whole rich tableau of history from mastodons to Muldoon. Even mastering this wasn't enough to make the Kiwi grade. Unlike my academic colleagues, I wasn't able to mend cars, build houses and play rugby—I still had nothing to talk about in the staff commonroom.

Unfortunately because specialists are so thin on the ground New Zealanders become suspicious of them. The all-rounder is preferred. Every year the country's part-owners pop in from the international pawnbrokers at the I.M.F. to inspect their pledge. Their dire warnings are always disregarded. After all, not one of them has handled a tool, even a screwdriver. In 1967 I did a television documentary attempting to analyse the Kiwi character. The audience was so shocked by my inability to put putty on a window that the brilliance of the argument was completely lost. Lack of practical skills is a form of personal inadequacy: as a perceptive correspondent in the *Woman's Weekly* once pointed out, 'protesters don't knit socks'. This adoration of the practical even influences the government hierarchy. In America the State Department carries the prestige, in Britain the Treasury. New Zealand esteems only the Ministry of Works whose minister can proclaim, 'My name is Ozymandias, king of kings: Look on my works ye Mighty, and despair!' to quote P. B. Allen, the Departmental Demosthenes pleading for a change of name to the Ministry of Good Works.

New Zealand owes much of its national character to the small-ness of the population. A mass society is hierarchical and frag-mented; a small one is uniform. Mass societies generalise into categories and classes; New Zealand deals in individuals, being small enough to particularise. Mass societies are preoccupied by abstractions and ideas: freedom, class, tyrannny, oppression. The Kiwi personalised society looks at people and their motives. If someone was declaiming about freedom and pri-vate enterprise an Englishman would listen. A New Zealander would quickly reduce it all to 'He's saying that because his father drank' or, if acquaintance is more distant, 'What's in it for him?' Continental workers strike against Gaullism, British against trade union legislation. The Kiwis' nearest approach to a political strike is against increased beer prices.* Instead of discussing ideas or grouping people into abstractions such as classes they prefer to gossip about individuals. Their national literature, like their conversation and women's magazines, is dominated by the 'funny thing that happened to me' ap-proach. A Briton would define someone by reference to some category, usually exact social position. The Kiwi does so by reference to his personal characteristics, usually his precise degree of 'good or bad blokiness'.

The same smallness also makes New Zealand a uniform, egalitarian society. Of course other factors help. There's no natural diversity. There are twenty-two breeds of sheep here but the humans mostly come from the same stock, are nearly all the same colour, have no deep social divisions and all go to the same schools. Minorities are too small to stand out. There is a small Chinese population but you'll have to hunt them out in the yellow pages, under G or L. Even the nine per cent who happen to be Maori don't break the uniformity. They usually segregate themselves in the countryside, in the plastic pas of Rotorua, or in the poorer areas of the cities

* See Fishopanhauser and Smith, 'Conflict Theory and Beer Prices in a Southland Town'. A Ph.D. thesis assessing the relevance of Action Theory to empirical political analysis, including an attempt to establish a basis for determining the relationship between individual behaviour and system attributes. Based on in-depth interviews with 250 drunks.

where no one sees them, though all claim to hear. Only a few young militants have shown any great desire to be exclusive or militant. Most are brown New Zealanders with larger families and different family customs. Their traditional leaders make Uncle Tom look like Eldridge Cleaver.

In any case New Zealand needs the Maori. He is the national fig leaf. The academics can study him, the artists pinch his motifs, and the liberals sympathise with him, even if he doesn't appear to understand what they are talking about. More important, as long as he's there a stretch of white suburbia whose attitudes are evocative of a Rhodesia without Africans can pose as multi-racial, racially tolerant and other nice things. The whole process is quite painless. The Maoris are just a large enough proportion to make the rest feel virtuous and not large enough to inconvenience them, unless they happen to live next door which none of those who talk about the Maoris ever do. The concession of equality is nicely self-interested. As long as the Maori has only equal rights and equal treatment, poverty and lack of education will make him incapable of competing effectively. No Maoris, no poor.

Even differences of wealth aren't really a source of diversity.* New Zealanders don't mind having the doctor in his castle, the patient at his gate, for financial equality is not enshrined in the Kiwi Pantheon. Because doctors are better unionised than wharfies they naturally deserve more: $7,000 a year more on average. Raising sheep is clearly more important than raising children so it's better paid. Producing beer is more praiseworthy than guzzling it, an act which demands only a reckless courage and a dulled sensitivity. Property also makes perfect. With rocketing values since the war farmers have clearly done well, even if things have got so tough now that some have been compelled to drive Jaguars over four years old. The owners of scrubby gullies near Auckland do even better. The most profitable crop to plant is still septic tanks.

The difference of wealth doesn't make a class system, because the country is so small. Concentration makes classes. In mass societies the like gather together, developing their own life styles, uniforms, newspapers and magazines, languages. Here Remuera and Fendalton look like a scruffy social hodgepodge compared with uni-class areas in London. The social groups are too scattered to congeal into classes. The British upper class has Fortnum and Masons to themselves. New Zealanders must forage in the Four Square. A New Zealand

---

* See H. Sheisenhauser and Les Cumberland, 'Status Attribution, Self Assigned Social Grouping, Inverse Social Mobility with Cognitive Dissidence and the Incidence of Plaster Ducks on Walls'. An exploratory survey based on 2.8 million random interviews with a stratified sample of New Zealanders. Condensed five-volume summary of results shortly available.

Tatler and Bystander could survive only by descending to photos of 'a happy family group exchanging blows at No. 34 State House Road, Grey Lynn'. Think of *Vogue, New Zealand*. After three thin years it had done features on the upper class (all four of them). Loath to turn to features on fashion among Wattie's cannery workers, it closed down. No one noticed.

This scatter factor prevents any like group gathering together for mutual encouragement and support. The only real Kiwi subculture is the seasonal subculture of students, which is why no one can stand them. In a North Island city a lone Trotskyite deviationist would like to test-drive a revolution with friends and bring his kids up in a commune. Instead the kids go to the local primary, his wife absorbs the *Weltanschauung* of the local newspaper and he has no one to talk to. In mass societies you know a few people deeply. Friends are picked on the basis of like backgrounds and attitudes. The Kiwi acquaintance is wide, not deep. They are all thrown together and they've got to get on together, so their skill is at keeping acquaintance as pleasant as it is shallow. To go deeper might tap well-springs of irreconcilable differences. Talk to the neighbour about the rose bed or the wife and you needn't worry whether he's a Maoist revolutionary, an ex-member of the Hungarian Iron Guard or one of the children from the Hutt Valley scandal of 1954, now grown prematurely old and doddery.

In this way the people manage to conceal what little diversity there is. They do so so well that they become positively anxious about diversity, if it ever crops up. A small society is an intimate one. Big Neighbour is always watching you. Keep him happy. Conform. Socially it is not advisable to get out of line or demonstrate any pretension, even were this possible in a society where money buys only a bigger car and a swimming pool, not a different accent, a uniform or an indefinable thing called 'style'. Pretension is, in any case, difficult where everyone knows you; 'he may be Director of the Reserve Bank, but I remember him picking his nose on the way to school'. For the same reason it is impossible for them to have any folk

heroes. Americans may revere Washington and Britons vener-
ate Churchill. New Zealanders would be too obsessed by the
fact that the one fiddled his expenses and the other drank too
much to respect their achievement. So the Monarch has to
live overseas. Kiwis have tried to establish local substitutes;
people in Timaru used to defer to a man they believed to
be an illegitimate son of Edward VII; people in Stewart
Island to an alleged granddaughter of Bonnie Prince Charlie.
Both places soon restored their allegiance to the House of
Windsor. If they in turn ever implemented the threat of more
frequent royal visits, the Kiwis would transfer again—to
Emperor Hirohito.

In a small country everyone knows if feet of clay exist. If
they don't New Zealanders will invent them. Kiwis have a
deep egalitarian drive, summed up in the law 'Thou shalt not
get up thyself'. This is a difficult feat anatomically but one
we see going on all the time, and anyone suspected of it
faces severe retribution. In Britain the mail of people exposed
on television consists of pleas for help, sexual advances and
requests to be cured of the King's Evil. Mine in New Zealand
was small and more likely to consist of anonymous vitupera-
tion, accusations of communist or fascist leanings (depending
on what day of the week it was), and suggestions to return to
Britain. Baron Charles Philip Hippolytus de Thierry, self-
styled 'Sovereign Chief of New Zealand', ended his sovereignty

giving piano lessons in Auckland. Rumour has it that one of New Zealand's baronets used to serve behind a bar, where patrons were invited to 'Drink Bellamy's Beer, Served by a Peer'.

Kirk's Law of Social Gravity states that the higher you go the more they will try to pull you down. If you are in an élite position you must disguise the fact in two ways. The first is to look as vacuous, illiterate and normal as the rest of the populace. A startled British High Commissioner once observed Sir Keith Holyoake 'declaring with pride that he was no intellectual, he was not well educated, he had left school when he was fourteen and had never been near a university'. The High Commissioner, of course, failed to realise that all this made Sir Keith peculiarly well fitted to be Prime Minister, just as a similar array of qualifications might well fit Mr Kirk for the same job. No New Zealand Prime Minister this century (with one* exception) has been near a university, unless to slip in by the back door to collect an honorary degree under plain cover. Few politicians have verged on the literary. There is no tradition of political alibiography; few even dare to leave letters for a historian to do his job of transferring bones from one graveyard to another. The second disguise is to eschew the prerogatives of office. Ministers' rooms must be open to every passing lunatic. Even the Prime Minister can't afford to ignore the Tapanui Women's Division. Peter Fraser used to show that running the war effort wasn't making him big-headed by popping out to inspect leaky roofs on state houses. Keith Holyoake has been known to find suitcases lost by indignant railway travellers. When I told this story to a French television crew they incredulously tested it by ringing the Prime Minister from their hotel room, film and tapes rolling. Anticlimax. A maid answered. Mr Holyoake was out. Could he ring them back? Our élite must behave in this fashion, not because they want to, but because otherwise they are certain to be accused of 'Uphimselfism'.

With socialists, equality is a matter of political principle,

* Two since Mr Marshall became P.M.

until they reach power, when it's a question of amnesia. In New Zealand it is a simple fact of group conformity. It is negative not positive. Its basis is a widespread feeling that if we can't all have something, no one should. Exceptions are made only for no-remittance cars and leprosy.

This is the country of 'the right thing'. When interviewers confront citizens in the street with microphones they are so anxious to say it that they all say the same thing. Give them a norm and they'll conform to it, unless its next name is Kirk. The process implies no belief in the norm, simply a considerate desire to avoid embarrassing others or discomforting themselves. Kiwis are virtuous; surveys of church attendances indicate that about a third go regularly, half once a month or more. They are also better ministered, at one per 500 adherents, than they are doctored. Yet all this is not through any yearning for salvation—they've got that already. It's a necessary indication of respectability. Kiwis are honest and law abiding not because they are moral; their approach to the Ten Commandments is like a student to his exam paper— only four to be attempted. Rather they don't want to step out of line. 'Thou shalt not be seen to' is more important than the actual 'Thou shalt not'.

Big Neighbour is always watching but his ability to enforce his whim comes from the others' guilt feelings, not his power. The cold-blooded and insensitive can do anything, simply by wearing a suit, attending the Jaycees and carting a prayer book round on Sunday, provided their orgies, drug parties and Red Book readings are kept behind closed doors.

Big Neighbour has positive sanctions only when two conditions are fulfilled. The act must be known. It must make people feel threatened. Then rumours will circulate, accusations will be launched in *Truth*, the telephone will make odd noises, ministers will announce in Parliament that you attended a meeting of the U.S.S.R. Friendship Society eighteen years ago. Friends and acquaintances will sidle up to assure you they 'don't believe a word of it' before dashing off to sudden, urgent appointments. The Great New Zealand Clobbering Machine will have trundled into action.

More normally there is a tolerant intolerance simply because of the intimacy. You can hardly be rude to someone you see every day, however many anonymous letters you might write to the press about him. And if intimacy is intolerant, it is also warm and friendly. This is the friendliest country in the world, a characteristic it is not advisable to question if you value your teeth. Everyone knows the story of General Freyberg driving through the New Zealand lines in the desert with a British general. 'Not much saluting is there,' says the highly pipped Pom. 'Ah yes, but if you wave they'll wave back.'

To make life even more pleasant New Zealand has one of the highest standards of living in the world: second in the car ownership league, fourth in telephones, third in washing machines, second in beer consumption at twenty-five gallons per fuddled capita, and first in tons of soap and number of showers per person. Many of the cars should be in motor museums, the phones don't have subscriber trunk dialling, the washing machines are prediluvian tubs, the beer is tasteless, and the soap is carbolic. It hardly matters. Wellbeing is more evenly shared here than anywhere else.

This has been achieved with unpromising raw materials. New Zealanders don't work like Germans, organise like Japanese, or compete like Americans. All they have is a practical flair. The country is too far from anywhere to be natural suppliers and too small to provide a worthwhile market for anyone else. It is too tiny to forge its own destinies and is subject to fluctuations beyond its control with massive internal political repercussions. But for this vulnerability the Continuous Ministry would still be in power (if this isn't in fact the case). The land has few minerals, just a certain amount of natural beauty waiting to be built on or flooded, and an ability to grow grass. The standard of living depends on the animals unimaginative enough to eat grass and on the world's willingness to eat them, though if the scientists have anything to do with it, they'll eat the wool, too, eventually. These are the only valuable exports, although in the past few years the nation has begun to develop a new line which can be expanded in emergency—the export of the limited range of fine quality, locally produced people. Well made New Zealand. And how pleasant the manufacturing process.

Casual observers, after that two-day stay which qualifies them as experts, often assume that the scale of New Zealand's achievement in the face of the inherent difficulties is the result of a deliberate pursuit of socialism. They call New Zealand the Land of the Long Pink Cloud, or Shroud depending on viewpoint. In fact it's all been done by accident. People settled there not to build a perfect society, but just to improve their lot. Since they came mainly from working and lower middle-class backgrounds their concept of what they wanted to achieve was the life-style of the groups immediately above them in Britain, the middle class. The goals were modest. (They have continued to think small.) And the methods were practical and workmanlike. There was no ideological plan— they just tinkered as they went along, reducing this little universe to order by organising and regulating it. Then they

set out to cut it off from the rest of the world as far as possible. Both methods helped shape the national character.

One of the greatest Kiwi skills is organising bureaucracies. Give them a problem and they'll set up a committee, or an organisation. They provide welfare through voluntary organisations, with mums forming play-group committees, parents forming P.T.As, Dads organising Rotaryisseries or Lion Packs (each desperately occupied in the despairing task of finding any poor and underprivileged to be charitable to). This is the welfare society. Above it hovers the greatest voluntary organisation of all, the State, which is seen as the community in action, rather than the remote abstraction it is elsewhere. The community wants a high and uniform standard of living. The State will provide it with two clever tricks. Full employment eliminates both poverty and the fear of being out of work and endows the people with their casual independence. Family allowances, state housing and welfare benefits also help to provide a level below which it is difficult to fall, a much simpler approach to welfare than President Nixon's policy of making it illegal to be poor, or the proposal by other American right-wingers to use nuclear weapons in the war on poverty.

Bureaucracy and regulation aren't enough. The New Zealander also has to live. If economic forces were free to operate, New Zealand would be three farms manned by a skeleton staff. The rest of the people would have to evacuate and leave the country to its rightful owners, Federated Farmers, with just enough others to service their Jaguars. Since there are three million New Zealanders, not just the 100,000 which economic logic would dictate, they have taken the protective measure of building a fence of tariffs and licences round the economy so that a pampered industry can develop.

This careful insulation has annoying consequences. Rabid sectional jealousies develop. Farmers exhibit acute pastoral paranoia when they see the rest of the populace lounging round demanding high wages at the expense of the only productive section (the sheep and the cows). Similarly, employers are bitter at workers who don't put in longer hours churning out items the market is too small to take. And farmers, employers, workers all combine into a chorus of grumbling about the welfare state, regulations, controls, restrictions and the result of the 3.30.

So vociferous is the chorus you might assume the country is on the brink of civil war or armed uprising. Indeed, large numbers of French arms salesmen went out there after the Biafra war, thinking to find their next potential customer. Also grumbling is a major political sport. Prizes are allocated for it; small ones like a post office or a new school for the short burst, big ones like protection or subsidies for a really sustained effort. The current grumbling league table puts doctors first in both volume and prizes, farmers second. Uni-

versity staffs are now moving up fast, having quickly mastered the art. Geographically it is only fair that Auckland should grow fastest. Its inhabitants have the loudest mouths for grumbling.

The second consequence is that private enterprise is more private than enterprising. It is inefficient. It carries on production in 9,000 small factories where a few big ones producing economically might be more sensible. Industry is expensive; television sets cost twice as much as Japanese imports, though bigger screens may be needed for larger people.

Yet the role of business isn't to produce cheaply, or efficiently, but to wangle concessions from the government. The most enterprising entrepreneur is he who gets the most support: grants, import licences, or protection. These are the key to profit, not production. Nevertheless the country does export some manufactured goods; in 1969 it even sent $17 worth of musical instruments to Cambodia.

Most of the manufactured exports are potential not real. Entrepreneur and ex-car salesman Ken Slabb wants to exploit the local market for left-handed corkscrews. The market is limited and small-scale production and an inordinate rate of profit will make his product eighty-four times more expensive than imports. The solution is to claim that his main aim is to export millions of left-handed corkscrews every year. With supporting evidence from Ken's great-uncle and an ex-girl-friend in Australia, poetic submissions are then heard by the Tariff, Development and Upholstery Council, where, despite opposition from the Glove, Mitten and Boottee Trade Association, the council agrees to exclude all left-handed corkscrews to give him a chance to establish himself. Within ten years the price of left-handed corkscrews has gone up 184 times, though sales have trebled because most of those used break on impact with a cork. Ken Slabb has made a fortune and retired to an island in the Bay of Islands, selling out to a British firm of corkscrew manufacturers who used to supply the market before he intervened. The exports have failed to materialise because of unfair trade practices on the part of the Australians and the unexpectedly heavy wage demands of the

New Zealand worker. The alternative ending to this story is that prices increase only 180 times and the manufacturer goes bankrupt.

This may horrify you. Visiting I.M.F. teams have been so numbed by it that they have been unable to say anything for months but the name 'Bill Sutch' repeated interminably. In fact, of course, New Zealand can live comfortably only by standing orthodox economics on its head. To understand the economic system you have to abandon what you've been brought up to regard as sense. Agricultural exports provide enough for all to live on. Kiwis could spend their time blowing bubbles or reading back numbers of *Playboy* were it not for some deep-seated puritan instinct which conditions them to want to work. So jobs have to be provided. Industry exists not to make *things* but to make *work*. The most efficient industry is the one which uses its labour most inefficiently; wharfies make their greatest contribution when seagulling; smokos do more for the economy than shift working. All the jokes about wharfies, like the one who complained to his foreman that a tortoise had been following him round all day, or the aerial photo of Wellington wharves which was ruined because a wharfie moved—all these miss the point. Work is like muck, no good unless its well spread.

Being practical men, New Zealanders are concerned not with hypothetical questions such as would Adam Smith, or even Robert McNamara, approve of our economy, but does it work? It does. The people have jobs, a good standard of living, a car and a lovely home each. Who could ask for more. They are not even concerned with the problem of whether the system could work better. Good enough is better than hypothetical perfection. Anyway the system works so well and has made the inhabitants so contented that they are the world's most stable, and probably most conservative society.

Seriously, New Zealand is the best place in the world to live. It is called God's Own Country. Modern theologians may argue whether God is dead. The rest of the world must pose him a lot of problems. Yet if the strain does get too much then he'll not die. He'll retire here.

STUPENDOUS, FANTASTIC, BEAUTIFUL NEW ZEALAND

(In Black and White)

DON'T THINK of New Zealand as a nation. It is an accidental collection of places whose inhabitants happen to live in much the same fashion and talk the same language; not so much a nation as more a way of life. How tenuous the connections are I realised on decimalisation day. A woman in a Christchurch shop announced that she wasn't going to bother with this decimalisation rubbish. They were moving to Invercargill next week. Dunedinites think of Auckland as another country. Aucklanders advise South-bound trippers to take enough overcoats and hot-water bottles for the South Pole. Interisland ferry sailings generate as much emotion as a world cruise. It's as though an umbilical was being severed. At both ends.

New Zealand is a collection of communities, not the metropolitan country you know. In France, Paris sets the tone and controls a centralised machinery of administration. In Japan, Tokyo dominates business and houses a substantial part of the population. In Britain, London dominates; television and newspapers originate there, the social whirl centres there and career ladders end there. New Zealand is different. There is not one main centre but four, and even together they contain only about a third of the population. They are also far apart and very jealous of each other. Even if they could develop collective pretensions they are all jealously watched by a league of little sisters. Oamaru and Invercargill won't stand for much from Dunedin except bad television programmes; Palmerston North keeps a close eye on Wellington. In any case the eighteen biggest urban areas contain just over half the population. All the other places have claims of their own, too.

In Britain everywhere outside London carries the stigma of being provincial. New Zealanders work on the assumption that all places are equal, though the growth of Auckland may have opened up the possibility that some are more equal than others. Life has a local focus. Different places view different television programmes, look at different newspapers and listen to different radio programmes. To be a Timaruvian means as much as to be a New Zealander. The only reason that travellers identify themselves overseas as New Zealanders is because no one seems to have heard of Waipukurau or Totaranui. Of course they draw together as a nation for the occasional catharsis—an All Black victory, a royal tour. Then they fall back into competing localities. This competition is all the more vigorous because it is one of the few notes of diversity in a uniform community.

Farmers live in the same kind of boxes as the rest; the boxes just happen to be in the middle of fields. Social habits are the same everywhere, though some have a longer drive to the pub. Nearly everybody looks out on the same jungle of tottering telegraph poles and tangled wires; there could be sewerage pipes to look at, too, if governments had been able to devise a safe method of stringing them among all the other dangling paraphernalia. New Zealanders are all campers on a lovely landscape and the main element of difference in their lives is the accident of which camp site they happen to have picked. Wherever it is, you must remember one basic rule: the place where you are now is the best in New Zealand, its people the friendliest, its streets the cleanest, its flower beds the prettiest. Everyone else is out to do it down. You must defend it to the last mixed metaphor against all criticism, however justified.

This state of affairs exists because every place is competing against every other. Parliament may go through routine motions of party debate but it only comes alive when it gets down to the real issues—the quality of the pies in the railway refreshment room at Clinton . . . whether Gisborne has got its fair share of Golden Kiwi grants as well as its more than fair share of everything else . . . would a chain and a twelve-pound ball encourage the doctor to stay in Hokianga . . . should the Christchurch City Council be allowed to plant concrete in Hagley Park. M.Ps aren't a national élite, they are local delegates, there to voice local demands.

Cabinets are similar. Indeed the requirements of geographical spread is the only conceivable explanation of the presence of some ministers, particularly ones from Dunedin. Cabinet decides the really important priorities. If Wanganui gets the eighteenth veterinary school, will the fourth college of chiropractors satisfy Hastings? If Auckland is to have a container port as well as an international airport, what can be done to conciliate Reefton's claim, short of rebuilding it on the coast? Perhaps a notional container port? For years governments have been praying for the ultimate dreams of localism, the garden shed university, the vertical take-off plane which can land anywhere and give everywhere an airport. Shortsightedly they have failed to realise that both would merely unleash even more bitter arguments by fragmenting parochialism into long wrangles over whose shed is to be used, whether the airport should go into the front garden or the back, who is to have the lemonade concession.

The parochial fight spills over everywhere. Imagine the fate of television directors exposed to constant demands to do a programme on Backblocksville, and then, if they do so, to constant threats ranging from pre-frontal lobotomy to castration because they didn't show the floral clock in the gardens. People connected with the old TV 'Compass' programme are still doing thirty-mile detours round Alexandra because a 1965 programme omitted to mention that it was the most beautiful town in New Zealand. Still, perhaps that's easier than the thirty-mile detour round everywhere else which would have been necessary if they had.

Imagine, too, the torments of royal tour itinerary planners, and the scandal which would have been produced if the private comment of one Governor-General that Oamaru and Timaru were like Tweedledum and Tweedledee had got out. Local government reform is impossible in a country where every place with more than a hundred people has to be a city, everywhere with more than five a borough, leaving to all the others the incentive to reproduce quickly. Local government is a system of dignity not function, conferring status on places and an elective honours list on the locally prominent. At 10,000 councillors and board members there are more *per capita magna* than anywhere else. In the smaller centres talk to everyone you meet as if he were the mayor. If you're wrong he'll certainly be on the council, unless you talk to yourself. The whole mistake of local government reformers has been to swim against the tide by trying to create bigger units and make mayoral chains lighter on the rates. A policy of 'Every man his own mayor' would be better.

Conversation has to make due deference to locality. Much of it is the routine exchange of stereotypes, decking out the petty struggle between localities in the trappings of romance. Every-

one in Dunedin wears a kilt. Everyone in Nelson has one eye. So here's a basic introduction which might help you to a better understanding, even if it does place me under the unfortunate obligation of mentioning every hamlet. The ultimate New Zealand book, and the best loved, is the Electoral Roll. The plot may be dull but everyone gets a mention.

Precedence among New Zealand cities goes to Auckland, believed by many, over a half a million in fact, to be the Queen City. Yet Auckland also has a large heterosexual population, even if there are some who believe that a pretty girl is like a malady. The city began as the sweepings of Sydney. Even now it has many of the characteristics of an Australia for beginners.

Auckland falls between two stools—too big for the rest of

New Zealand, too small to provide a genuinely big city existence. It is essentially a main street surrounded by thirty square
miles of rectangular boxes, covering as great an area as
London to far less purpose. Yet size is still the key to Auckland. It confers pretensions: the morning paper modestly takes
the name of the whole country, wealth seems easier to come
by and is certainly more flamboyant. This is a city of self-
made men who worship their creator. Its Joneses are more
difficult to keep up with. One can only be thankful that Auckland isn't actually the capital. With this further dignity its
inhabitants would be insufferable. Even now the snowball
processes of growth make Auckland almost unbearable, as well
as threatening to shatter the precarious federal balance that is
New Zealand.

Size also means that Auckland is a self-sufficient universe,
labouring under the delusion that the rest of New Zealand
doesn't exist and hence immersed in its own struggles and
conflicts. Its academic squabbles are more bitter: anyone from
the university can be kept going for hours just by mentioning
his colleagues; a putting in of pennies which produces a
constant stream of denunciation. The city's local government
disputes are more intense. Its M.Ps hate each other too much
to work together. Even the weather is undependable and
extreme. One TV meteorologist had to move south because the
weather didn't agree with him.

Auckland is a collection of suburbs masquerading as a city.
Wellington is a city centre without suburbs. They are all
thoughtfully hidden away round in Rongotai, over the hills
in Kelburn, or in the isolation ward of the Hutt Valley and
its satellites such as Wainuiomata (or Nappy Valley as the
locals have it). The suburbs are all several traffic jams away
from the ultimate traffic jam in the centre. Wellington was
designed as a capital city, but unfortunately its site wasn't.
The curving streets seem to mark the place the tide washed
the surveyors' pegs to. Even the Hutt Valley motorway can't
obviate the fact that if God had intended Wellington for
traffic he would have put it in Petone. So the motorway simply
speeds traffic more quickly to the central jam.

If the steep hills clustering round the harbour make Wellington a little inconvenient for all but Sherpas, they also make it beautiful. Man's attempts to ruin the scene by building in the monolithic style of the Maginot Line have hardly spoiled a view which must make it the world's most pleasant capital city. As a capital it has the institutions of government, administration and diplomacy all concentrated in the central area. Auckland has the pretension and the glory, Wellington the power. It lacks the colour, for Wellington is a public servants' town, a place to which the able and ambitious in the service must ultimately go. This makes for guarded conversation after the Rabelaisian overtones of Auckland, drab dress, but a more vigorous cultural life and schools whose children have the highest average I.Q. outside Midwitch. The tone is lowered only by the unfortunate fact that for half of the year Parliament meets, M.Ps pour in every Tuesday, and with them the attendant circus of delegations, representations and the ritual passing of begging bowls.

Still Wellington should be a truly beautiful city, if they ever finish building it. There is always the danger of earthquake but probably this is a slightly less appalling threat than that posed by the Ministry of Works. In any case Wellington could

quickly and easily be given complete protection against nuclear attack from the air. All they have to do is paint a huge arrow on the roof of the Vogel Building with the simple legend, 'To Auckland'.

Further south, Christchurch, City of the Plain, though more perceptively described as the swamp city. Christchurch likes to think of itself as an English city. This is partly because of the gardens and the presence of the Avon meandering through in its half-hearted search for the sea. It is also because of institutions such as the Cathedral, the private schools, the *Press* and the Medbury Hamburger Bar. In fact its town plan of straight lines leading nowhere and its flat, drab appearance both combine to make it more like a wild west town built in stone. John Wayne would almost certainly have hired it as a set for his westerns had the municipality been able to devise some way of joining the parking meters together to form hitching rails.

Christchurch is really English only in its social segregation. The ability to sprawl in any direction has allowed segregation by suburb in a way that the hilly sites and the jostling mixtures of Wellington and Dunedin have not permitted. Professionals work in Hereford Street making fortunes and they live in Cashmere or Fendalton (where the camel hair coat went to die). The remaining suburbs are nicely graded. Any estate agent will guide you to the appropriate one once you've told how much you can afford to pay over what you can afford to pay. If he suggests Sydenham or New Brighton you should start thinking of a new job. The latter has a run-down atmosphere and gawping icecream-eating crowds doing their Saturday shopping. It also houses more cranks to the acre than any other part of the country.

With this social segregation, its insularity and introspection and the general stodginess of the little interlocking group who rule the city, Christchurch must be the least pleasant of the main centres. Yet I'm tolerant enough to believe that other people may think differently. Perhaps the real symbol of Christchurch is the railway station, pretentious and monolithic, yet with only about half a dozen trains a day that go anywhere beyond Christchurch suburbs, and only the *Southerner* that really goes at all. This train provides the best view of Christchurch.

Dunedin, the semi-sunkissed city, is symbolised by its long uncompleted Anglican cathedral: impressive in conception, solid in execution yet incomplete and left standing half finished for decades. The little town that Santa Claus forgot sits near the bottom of the South Island and of every growth table. Outwardly pretending that the wolf at the door is a lucky black cat it is really characterised by a militant inferiority complex. Or rather its official organs and leaders are. The mass of the population don't care, finding it a pleasant place to live and so much less expensive than real life.

None of the conventional images of Dunedin are true. It is a university town only in the sense that the university bulks large in a city where it is the only expanding industry. The real relationship is symbolised by the moat round the Scottish Baronial Gothic. Scottishness means only that the import-restricted haggis puts in an occasional appearance and an occasional poet produces third-degree Burns. It is Presbyterian only in that the reverberating echoes of a small centre enforce conformity. Even so it manages an enviable reputation for provision of whatever favours sailors favour. It still gets more than its fair share of *Truth* reports, even since the demise of the Quartier Latin, Maclaggan Street. Psychologically and weatherwise Dunedin is a city of myths. Still it has more memories and fatter history books than anywhere else. These are some comfort to a city living in reduced circumstances with the feeling that life is passing it by.

By Seath's Law, parochialism varies in inverse ratio to size. Auckland and Christchurch are big enough to be confident and know they'll grow, whatever governments decide or pressure groups urge. Dunedin has to be more clamorous in the hope that hysteria will rectify the obstacles an inconsiderate nature has placed in the path of development.

The jostling second division of thirteen smaller centres ranging from Hamilton and Palmerston North down to Gisborne and Whangarei need to be more vocal still. Lacking

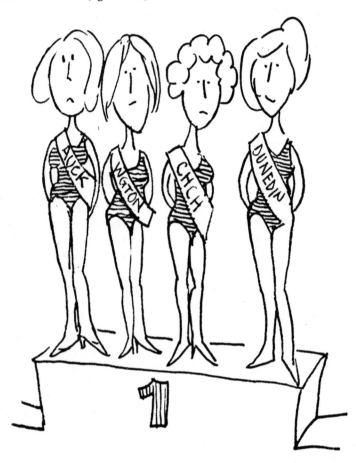

main centre status they clamour for the outward and visible signs of city stature—a university, a new airport, a Government Life building, a railway, a piecart. Insecurity is heightened by the unconscious realisation that no matter how they grow they're all irredeemably towns not cities. Links with hinterlands are stronger, urban identity weaker, life rawer and culture more consciously created. The intellectual élite of teachers, administrators and professional men are all consciously in exile, anxiously tilling the cultural desert around them. After-dinner speakers are hard to attract because it is customary to say something nice about the town they are speaking in. University staff are easier because they get mileage. In my days as an itinerant academic jukebox, visits to Invercargill, Nelson or Palmerston North gave me an insight into how St Augustine must have felt, so assiduously did the intellectuals present hang on to my words. Initially I put it down to the brilliance of the lecture. Later I realised that there wasn't much else for the four of them to do.

Secondary centres are in the unhappy position of not being big enough to have the compensations of real cities, yet not being small enough to have the quiet contentment of the real focus of New Zealand life: the small towns. Through these runs the great dividing line between the urban and the rural. The smaller the place the greater the importance of rural values, the more local services depend on the farmer, and the more his income determines the cash flow into the community. The more, too, that rural values and attitudes predominate.

There are regional differences. There is the slowly awakening Northland; the declining glories of the West Coast where men are larger than life and twice as tipsy and the New Zealand myths crawl away to die. At the other extreme are the gentry pretensions of Hawke's Bay and North Canterbury. Cow areas differ from sheep, not as Oliver Duff thought because sheep make gentlemen and cows unmake them, but because sheep make money, $1,000 per farmer more than cows. Cows not only provide lower average churnings, they also demand more attention from the 'moaners on the mud-flats'. The sheep farmer has more leisure, a different life style. Fruit and tobacco areas are different again: heavy demands for seasonal labour make Nelson and Hawke's Bay agricultural factories at certain times of the year. Small holdings and subdivision make parts of the Maori east coast more of a rural slum.

Whatever the regional differences, the pattern of life is similar in all the small centres: intimate communities in which everyone knows everyone else and their business even better. They are warm and friendly, tolerant of human frailty (like the odd wife with a black eye, the occasional pregnant daughter), though prepared to talk about it endlessly afterwards. They are family communities, middle-aged in values and attitudes. The young move on for jobs and education. The outsider assumes there is nothing to do in these one-horse towns—in fact there is everything. Voluntary activity runs all, from church groups to those high points of the year, the races and the A. and P. shows. The farmers till the land, their wives cultivate the wilderness of leisure.

These small towns are the real New Zealand, nurturing the values of warmth and friendliness and an endless interest in personal trivia. They set the tone for the whole nation. The attitudes, perspectives, institutions are those of the small town writ large. Parliament is the small town forum, the national equivalent of pub exchanges. The friendly neighbourhood security service under Brigadier Keystone also plays an allotted role, although it couldn't find a communist plot if it were stood on Lenin's grave. Its number is in the phone book so that you can always ring up and turn in your friends for fun and profit. Like the village Nosy Parker its job is to gather information. It is an institutional Big Neighbour.

Even the New Zealander's reaction to the nuisance of dissent is the same as the small town threatened with something out of the ordinary. The New Zealand Clobbering Machine is the national equivalent of small town community pressures. The things people are least happy about, political parties, class conflict, organised protest and dissent—these are just the things which don't exist in the small town so the folk can neither understand nor accept them.

So think of New Zealand as a small town with the trimmings of a nation state. Seriously though, you must admit that this small town tone makes for a friendly personal atmosphere as distinct from the impersonal anonymity you've left behind. And if you don't like it, keep quiet. You might be run out of town—on Air New Zealand.

EDUCATION:
The Making of the Resident

AN OXFORD college head once assured me that all New Zealanders look alike: tall, craggy featured, nothing to say. If he was right it must be because they are produced by standdardised processes, one of the most uniform production systems in the world outside die stamping. And thorough. New Zealanders spend as much time and trouble on raising young New Zealanders as they do on sheep. They can't spend as much money, but the people aren't intended for export.

The family is the basic unit of production, but you have to make allowances for it. Rearing New Zealanders is too important to be left entirely to families, who could, after all, include English immigrants, Labour voters and undetected libertarians. So all the way up the line the product is processed in government plants during the day and shuttled back to the home storage units at night and weekends.

In the beginning is the hospital. Babies have to be born there so that regular feeding can programme them to wake Mum at regular intervals and she can be made to feel guilty about such anti-New Zealand habits as sleeping after six a.m. or getting too much pleasure out of a child. Dad's exclusion from the process of birth and his grudging admission to the hospital conditions him to the view that the whole business has nothing to do with him. His job is restricted to waving rattles before unseeing eyes and going 'Goo-goo'. Neither his role nor his ability to communicate with his children ever improves much.

After hospital the Plunket Society, a paediatric Farm Advisory Service, steps in to reinforce the lessons. Its purpose is to check the spread of permissiveness and plastic pants among children under one by propagating the principles of child rearing common in advanced circles only fifty years ago. These rules were set out by Dr Truby King in his book *Scouting For Mothers*. Children should be a duty not a pleasure. Mum must not be allowed to bring up children in the way she wants. Parents should be seen and not heard.

Orwell's *1984* had a television camera in every room. New Zealand uses an inspectorate of Plunket ladies observing home practices, administering gentle correction where necessary. They are kinder to the children than to mothers. Plunket reports will surely be weighed in the scales of heaven, so they must be charitable. One day my daughter screamed continuously, bit the nurse and deposited what should have gone into the nappy in her lap. The record card commented mildly, 'An independent wee soul'.

A former Governor-General pointed out that 'if it were not for the success of the Plunket Society there might be no All Blacks'. There would be no Progressive Youth Movement either. The society makes New Zealanders what they are. It begins the lifelong tension between what we want to do and what we are conditioned to feel we *should* do. Young Everidge wants to eat when he's hungry; he's conditioned to nibble at four-hour intervals. He wants to play with himself; his hand gets slapped to show him sex is a dirty pleasure, suitable only for the dark. As a former Obergruppenführer of the Plunket Society once said, 'Give me the child for seven months, with whatever donations you can afford, and I will give you the All Black.'

In case conditioning fades, there is an after-sales service from 250 kindergartens and 300 play groups. These socialise the children to play together, but only incidentally. The main purpose is to give the mums something to do. These places are an outlet for that frenzied organisational drive which is the first symptom of postpuerperal depression, a chance to trade in old gossip for new and an opportunity to keep a wary eye on everyone else's child-rearing procedures. Is Sandra Binns's toilet training late? Her mum will be made to feel anxious. Does Johnny Jones go in for full frontal nudity? After all, the children won't be really happy unless they're exactly like everyone else.

This is also the view of the Department of Education, the intellectual branch of Sir James Wattie and company. Overseas they think of education as a process, a liberation, a joyous awakening. Such emancipation hardly fits in with the New

4

Zealand skill of regulation. It would produce a storm of protest from parents puzzled that their children should reject a life style they themselves have known from time immemorial (i.e. 1935). So this country has changed the meaning of the word. Education means a department, seeing that all plants produce to the same standard, turning a process of emancipation into a means of integration. So no one wants any.

The basic function of any government department is to keep its field of operations quiet. Education clings to this rule all the more anxiously, since its one aberration revealed the dangers of an alternative course. In 1935 Labour appointed a Minister of Education who was interested in the subject, had ideas and could push them through Cabinet— all factors which would have disqualified him for the job in normal circumstances. Peter Fraser and Dr Beeby initiated a primary school revolution. The authoritarian ethos was weakened. The insistence on the three Rs of reading, riting and rigidity was replaced by an effort to capitalise on the child's instinct to learn. Dr Dewey came to New Zealand to be embalmed in state.

The effort was too much. The revolution exhausted itself on the primary schools before it could reach the rigidly conservative postprimary schools. Now, a slightly archaic and staid liberalism of the primary system sits in schizophrenic contrast with a postprimary system, where instruction is handed down to be duly carved on tablets of stone.

The backlog of hostility from an older generation which had not enjoyed its own schooling and was determined that no one else should, made further innovations impossible. The collapse of morals, the untidiness of state house gardens and the growing incidence of public nose-picking were all authoritatively attributed to 'play-way'. Dr Beeby was sent off to be New Zealand ambassador to the Folies Bergère. The Department confined itself to administration. Since it is now largely manned by ex-teachers, the present system is safe and self-perpetuating. Those who can, teach; those who can't, administer. Those who can do neither become ministers.

As a final safeguard, education is administered by a complex balance of groups, so nicely deadlocked as to make change impossible. Boards are in friction with the Department, headmasters with boards, staffs with all three, school committees and P.T.As with any two at random. At the top of this house of cards sits the Minister, whose main qualifications are usually his complete inability to get anything through Cabinet and his enthusiasm for those educational techniques common in the late nineteenth century. In this way everyone in education can be left to fight everyone else so that the rest of the population can spend their money on booze, baccy and betting and the Government can go out shopping for frigates.

From the primary plant, young Kiwi-chile passes on to the intermediate school to reach puberty in decent purdah. He then enters a postprimary system divided into three parts— Catholic, Private or State. Catholic schools segregate the members of the faith and provide an inferior education suited to a minority of a seventh of the population. Private schools

(the National Party at lessons) do much the same for the better-off. Most pay a nominal allegiance to a religious denomination and a more real one to the eternal values represented by the A.N.Z. Bank. They are preparatory departments for Federated Farmers, providing boarding accommodation and reasonable restraint for country children. The more important, Christ's, King's and Wanganui Collegiate, are instant public schools, die-stamping little Englishmen under licence. Their female counterparts also produce some splendid chaps.

The more pretentious take English or religious names: St Margaret's after the wife of the founder of F. W. Woolworth, Christ's after the founder of the Church of England, Medbury Preparatory after the inventor of the hamburger. Most were founded in the mists of antiquity, like Southwell, starting in 1911 on endowment from the Sergel family, which still provides donations in the shape of a headmaster and children. Educational techniques which trained administrators for the British Empire and other Offshore Funds are applied by hand to a miscellaneous collection of offspring of farmers, lawyers and used-car salesmen (the country's second oldest profession). This gives the well-off something to spend their money on besides overseas trips. It also guarantees that their offspring won't be embarrassed by coeducation. All relatively harmless, since New Zealand is not an élitist society. The private schools can't yet take in E.S.N. children of the wealthy at one end and churn out directors for I.C.I. (N.Z.) at the other.

Because the private schools use their privacy to uphold a traditional education, the state schools have to do the same so parents won't divert their children *en masse*. As a new country, New Zealand is a great respecter of tradition and the schools which carry the most prestige are the most rigidly pedagogic. Places like Wellington Girls, Christchurch Boys and Waikukumukau Hermaphrodites set the tone. All the others have to try to keep back with them, so that parents don't think their children are being deprived.

By and large, which most of our children are, Joe Soap and Julian Unilever go to the same school. This is so that they can both start with equal disadvantages in life. For the army the schools are an excellent preparation. For life, not so good. New Zealanders are a lackadaisical, easygoing people: they educate their children by formalised pedagogy. Their dress is sloppy and casual: they impose a school uniform designed to kill all sexual interest by skilfully relandscaping burgeoning teenage shapes into mobile marquees. An open, democratic society, New Zealand has an authoritarian education system. The teacher is society's N.C.O., enforcing the virtues of obedience by corporal punishment or accrediting. Society is egalitarian, so the schools stream rigidly. Kiwis are a practical bunch of jokers, so the schools are obsessively academic. All this has been carefully thought out to nurture the latent schizophrenia in the Kiwi breast, programming him to feel guilty and uneasy about everything that is good. Puritan instinct demands that those who live in paradise should not enjoy it.

The doses of guilt aren't equally shared out. Manual workers and the less intelligent build up antibodies to the system. It conditions them to a cynicism about an education so uniquely irrelevant to their life experience and about authority figures who transmit on such an alien frequency. They leave school at the earliest possible opportunity and make money on the wharves, or rather less as Prime Minister or Leader of the Opposition. For the rest of their lives they are defiantly anti-intellectual. With the middle classes, the education system has deeper penetration, processing them into Boy Scouts who spend the rest of their lives looking for a movement, in such substitutes as Lions or Jaycees. Unfitted to enjoy paradise, they become deeply suspicious of those who do. The worst affected cases go on to the teachers' colleges, the technical institutes and the universities for a really concentrated dose of educational schizophrenia.

When you think of further education, the red brick, the white tile, or the Dulux ivory towers of Britain's universities spring to mind. Forget it. New Zealand has 4.3 universities and a number of training colleges and technical institutes which between them take, say, ten per cent of school leavers. They are all finishing schools for various professions, a job training for those who can't get it on the job. The lower grades—primary school teachers and lesser breeds without the law—go to the educational ghettos. The rest go to the universities, and the difference between the institutions is solely one of degree. The universities embrace not only Classics (production quota as set by the Development Conference, 34.5 a year) but also Physical Education and the Home Science School (the Dean of the Home Science School is the equivalent of your Warden of All Souls; the school's main role at the moment is to ensure that doctors' wives can cook). Flower arrangement would also be eligible for a degree course if the Women's Division didn't already do it so well. Being a practical people, the New Zealanders don't like to train intelligence at large; they have no tradition of taking philosophy graduates and putting them in charge of the Department of Marine, or appointing experts in the romance languages to run New Zealand Breweries. Studies have to be relevant to a career. Like freezing works, universities must produce visible returns in an annual crop of frozen teachers, accountants and engineers.

The universities have several advantages. Because of the tradition of going to the nearest university rather than the best, a high proportion of students live at home. Thus lots of them concentrate money on essentials, rather than lavishing it on accommodation. Universities are open to a larger proportion of the population than is the case in Britain: entry conditions are easier. Everyone has the right to fail once they're 21 and part-time study provides a people's democracy degree.

Unfortunately these New Zealand institutions are manned by an alien fifth column. One third of the staff come from overseas, mainly from Britain, where universities are very different creatures. The most able British academics wouldn't dream of coming to a country they regard as an academic outer Siberia. In 1959 I would have been hard put to get a job as assistant janitor at Battersea Polytechnic. In New Zealand I was a full lecturer. Promotion is so rapid that most people finish up as Associate Professor. Unfortunately their inability to get jobs in British universities makes importees more anxious and assertive about a university status they hold so tenuously.

A high proportion of the natives have also been corrupted by postgraduate training overseas. The most able are lost, unable to stand the loneliness of the long-distance intellectual and the lack of stimulus and excitement. The only section genuinely appreciative of the country's traditions is the small but increasing number of Americans, bomb refugees, Vietnam protesters and people unwilling to buy a second-hand America from President Nixon. Since many of them are busily building bomb shelters, lobbying for peace or supporting student revolt they are collectively dismissed as insane, politically unstable or both.

With this exception, university staffs spend their time complaining because their intellectual gifts are not recognised by

the community in general and Mr Muldoon in particular, lamenting at the government's failure to pay them as much as American and British academics, and airing their highly developed God complexes on their students. The only way in which they resemble good New Zealanders is their nine to five work habits and their quiet domesticity in the better suburbs like Cashmere, of which the University of Canterbury poet said, 'I will lift up mine eyes to the hills, whence cometh my staff'.

The students are another ground for staff dissatisfaction. They take the books out of the library, make the place look untidy, drive suspiciously close to the staff when homeward bound. The staff want to teach only the best but have to drop their artificial pearls in front of swine. The staff want students to be passionately interested in their subject; the students want a meal ticket and will put together any kit-set structure of Wisdom I, Taste and Discrimination II and Sense and Sensibility III which puts them as quickly as possible on to the labour market. The staff want excitement and

discussion from students whose schooling has prepared them only to take down sacred texts. Say 'Good morning' to a class of British students and they'll reply, 'Good morning, Comrade'. Say it in New Zealand and they'll take it down. The lecturer's approach has to be to say what he's going to say, say it, then recapitulate—a lesson brought home to me in my first lecture. With a naive enthusiasm for Socratic techniques, I outlined the case of those who thought the gentry rose from 1540-1640, then the counter case against the self-raising gentry, and invited them to choose. I was surrounded by an anxious group of students asking, 'But what do you think?' Here was the key to success and the line that would come back to me, with some deterioration in the grammar and style, in exam papers.

Staff see students as a necessary nuisance and a numerical argument for increased finance for their department. For university authorities the students are another problem. University officials want a quiet life, an undisturbed production flow of books, articles and graduates, and a happy local community which will hand over large sums of money because its clean, well scrubbed students are almost as big a tourist attraction as the botanical gardens. Unfortunately the raw material is volatile: girls get pregnant, students demonstrate instead of leaving it to lab assistants. Even the capping celebrations, whose real purpose is to give lawyers a week they can talk about for the rest of their lives, get embarrassing. The proper response is to turn the universities into custodial institutions, putting up the sign 'Abandon home all ye who enter here' and setting up halls of residence as an institutional chastity belt.

The staff are kept under control by the need to compete for scarce resources. Most departments are run on a slender secretarial staff, usually a brunette. They are understaffed and can't finance research projects. Staff want new premises, sabbatical leave, or a trip to a conference in Australia. So all are controlled by the constant need to lobby, to propitiate and to please. University staff abandon ambitions of being good academics and concentrate on being petty lobbyists and empire builders. The best brains in the university are absorbed in a self-generating process of committee work, caucusing and canvassing. Having thus ensured a quiescent staff, Vice-Chancellors can get on with their real jobs: making speeches about the Muldoon threat to intellectual integrity, lobbying for appointment to the Broadcasting Corporation, deciding whether to refer the Capping Magazine to the Indecent Publications Tribunal, or applying for jobs overseas.

The universities should do four jobs. First, they need to expand and order the body of knowledge. They do this now, but achieve an output of only 0.8 articles per capita per year, and that mainly by taking overseas experiments and research and duplicating them in New Zealand. With a little more productivity and a bit more attention to New Zealand subjects, all would be well. Even the second job of communicating knowledge retail to the detainees is well enough done, though the aerosol approach is preferred to the hand polishing Oxford considers appropriate.

The third job is to turn out, not working models of professional men on to whom a little knowledge has been grafted without immediate rejection effects, but intellectuals, people whose thirst for knowledge is like an addiction. The universities don't attempt this. The public image of students is of ignorant, drug crazed militants. In practice most are quietly conformist: in the years I was one of the trustees of the De Tocqueville Fund, to award an annual prize of $200 for the biggest insult to authority in any year, we never had one entrant, beyond a case of accidental pant wetting at a north Dunedin kindergarten. Students are drawn overwhelmingly from middle class backgrounds, with as few as a fifth from manual working homes, a proportion only double the contingent from overseas. Thus background insulates them from the infection of new ideas. Staff-student contact is minimal. Where it exists it is largely confined to the one department: in a survey only one in ten had had contact with staff from another department. Cross-sterilisation seems more appropriate than cross-fertilisation.

A last role—spreading knowledge out into the community —is scarcely attempted. Few are more academically snobbish and purist than the academically dull. Even the academic branch of show biz, so flourishing in Britain, does not exist. The University of Canterbury viewed my television appearances as if I was running a house of ill-fame on the side. New Zealand universities are inward-looking, preoccupied with themselves, isolated from a community which desperately needs the information, the ideas and the stimulus and diversity universities could provide. Unfortunately to do so might upset people.

Seriously though, these universities are the best in the world. Don't ask the students, they're biased. If you don't believe me, ask the staff. You'll find them either doing their gardens or Post Restante, c/o University of London.

THE KIWI SCIENCE OF POLITICS

THERE ARE SOME aspects of life in your new home I've hesitated to talk about. People who let their gardens get overgrown, Invercargill, bodily odours—all these had to be left until you are strong enough to bear the shock. So had politics.

In God-Zone you approach different topics with an adjustment of your volume control. With sport, shout; with sex, whisper; with politics, mutter. America's silent majority is New Zealand's muttering majority. If you're afflicted by that rare perversion, a passion for politics, you'll have to mutter more than a German with a severe Oedipus complex.

In the small amount of spare time they have left over from their main job of defending themselves against Mr Muldoon (the Genghis Khan of finance), the political scientists have been able to write numerous books and articles. By Mitchell's Law, as the life goes out of politics it is replaced by analysis. This simple rule of taxidermy means that the duller politics become, the more frenzied and sophisticated is the attention that the burgeoning profession of political science devotes to the corpse. Voting turn-out down—analysis of elections up.

You will look in vain for the rapier shaft of wit which, in

overseas systems, has produced such classics as 'the thousand best jokes of Richard Nixon, the Abraham Lincoln of North Vietnam', or 'the wit of Edward Heath, the Bexley Bismarck'. You won't find the sense of style which lyrical public relations men conferred on President Kennedy ('with new DIGNITY!'), or even the ersatz version the early Harold Wilson ('You don't use Wilson—Wilson uses you!') had, until the aerosol ran out. True, Brian Talboys was run for a few months as an import substitute Jack Kennedy (it's amazing what they can do with silicones), but he was too good-looking. Nor will you discover new philosophical insights. 'The Thoughts of Chairman Keith' have not yet joined those other slim volumes, *Italian War Heroes* and *Arab Victories,* in published form. There's no 'Kirk on Political Theory', and 'Linear Demand Coefficients in Econometric Predictive Models' by R. D. Muldoon has yet to hit the waiting world. The people have rugby for national catharses, and assassination of politicians has never caught on here. Ignoring them is so much more effective.

Politics is best compared with the septic tank. Septic tanks have no tradition: they are plumbed in with the house. Septic tanks have no elegance and no wit, though you may get the occasional gurgle. You don't talk much about septic tanks. They burble along nicely with a triennial overhaul. Yet they do serve a certain purpose.

Most countries have only one system of government. Just as a high standard of living gives New Zealand more consumer durables than other countries, so it gives more systems of

government per capita. On the latest count, there are four, changed in regular rotation with the seasons, like vests.

In January there is neither system nor government. Everything must stop for the summer break. If, by some divine oversight, the second coming falls due at this time of year, a third and final appearance will certainly be necessary to transfer Kiwis to another (and possibly inferior) heaven. In January such a happening would be as little noticed as licensing laws on the West Coast in the old six o'clock closing days. You may find it surprising that revolutionaries don't take the opportunity offered by this interregnum to take power and seize the reins. No real danger. Thoughtful immigration laws keep out people like Tariq Ali or Cohn-Bendit, excluding brown, pink and yellow with equal impartiality. And the local revolutionaries are all dinkum Kiwi. In January they're on holiday, the one at Ninety Mile Beach, the other on his power boat at Taupo.

In February the country slips into its totalitarian phase,

which lasts until May. Cabinet meets busily, its working hours coinciding neatly with the old pub opening times (which Orthodox boozers still keep, even if the Reformed Brethren don't). To remain busy in the lunch break, the ministers put on morning suits, transforming themselves into the Executive Council, or Cabinet sitting pretty. On days Cabinet does not meet, ministers while away the time with tours of the country finding out what their departments are doing, or where they are. A minister's ability is usually measured by his mileage.

These are the months of decision, when the beehive buzzes with activity. Import licensing is imposed or taken off. Subsidies are abolished. Controversial decisions are announced, usually on a Friday night so that newspapers, printed without journalists on Saturday and Sunday, can deal with them only when they're dead issues. Troops are dispatched to wherever our allies (collectively known as the logic of destiny) would like them to go—usually Southeast Asia, an area the Kiwis are anxious to make safe for mutton. It's moments like these we need SEATO.

All decisions are unchallenged. Parliament stands silent or is hired out to international organisations needing a veneer of respectability for their gatherings. The Opposition hibernates in some undiscovered retreat in the South Island. Both Parliament and the Opposition will discuss all in due course, but so late that the debate will have the compelling fascination of a postmortem on a body several months putrescent.

From May to December the nation takes on the trappings of Parliamentary Democracy. Stroll down to the House and along the corridors of power, with the rattling floorboards specially designed by the security service to give warning of arriving assassins. The Parliamentary traditions you will find are those of Burke and Hare rather than Burke and Fox. When interest was greater the country could support a double feature in the General Assembly (R.18) and the Legislative Council (R.75), a political geriatric ward. In a memorable debate this last chamber once debated a proposal to enhance the tourist attractions of Dunedin and give pleasure to the local Italian population (Sig. Giuseppe Martini, 1 Michie St, Roslyn) by buying a dozen gondolas to use on the harbour before it silted over. Ever conscious of the need for economy, always a pressing consideration with Otago estimates, one elderly councillor rose from his slumbers to move an amendment to buy not twelve gondolas but just a male and a female and let nature take its course.

The House is similar—witness this scintillating exchange between Sir Sidney Holland, believed to have been Prime Minister, and Mr Hackett, who may have been a spokesman of the New Zealand Federation of Hairdressers and Dental Surgeons:

> Mr Holland said that the country was getting good value for the money spent on the police force. What other workers worked overtime without any special pay he asked?
> Mr Hackett: Nurses in hospitals.
> Mr Holland: They are not policemen. (*Dominion* 26 October 1956.)

Demosthenes would not have been allowed to enter New Zealand but his traditions are well maintained. Listen to this polished oratory from a former Minister, Mr W. J. Scott:

> 'Part II of the proposed regulations deals with the operation of fish farms. Regulation 15 declares that a licensee of a fish farm may lawfully be in possession of or sell or dispose of fish he has raised on the farm, but subject to the provisions of the regulations. Regulation 16 provides that a licensee may have on his farm only fish which have been raised on the farm or lawfully transferred to the farm and that a transfer can take place only with the authority of the Secretary for Marine. Regulation 17 prohibits a licensee from canning fish or being in possession of fish in cans which have been raised on his farm.' (*Parliamentary Debates*, 1 October 1969.)

Oratory is complemented by a deftness of repartee which would have gladdened the heart of Disraeli and his straight man, Gladstone:

> Mr Walker: I am reminded of the occasion when he was most critical in this House about rates going up in Christchurch . . . on the night the rates were discussed by Christchurch City Council the honourable member had leave to go to the Labour Party Ball.

Hon. R. M. Macfarlane: I did not go to that ball.

Mr Walker: Well, the member was not at that meeting.

Mr Hunt: That is absolutely untrue and the member knows it.

Mr Holland: A point of order, Mr Speaker. I draw your attention to the fact that the member for New Lynn interjected saying that what the member said was perfectly untrue and the member knew it.

Mr Speaker: Is that what the member said?

Mr Hunt: Not exactly. I said it was absolutely untrue.

Mr Walker: Experience throughout the world has shown that properties adjacent to a motorway increase in price when the motorway is completed.

Hon. H. Watt: That is a lot of rubbish.

Mr Walker: Property adjacent to a motorway increases in value (interruption).

Mr Speaker: Order. We should not have more than ten people speaking at once.

Mr Walker: I should like to hear the Deputy Leader of the Opposition deny that.

Hon H. Watt: I deny it.

Mr Walker: I should like to hear him deny that Memorial Avenue in Christchurch . . . .

Hon. H. Watt: That is not a motorway.

Mr Walker: It is a mini-motorway.

Such is the lightning flash of free debate and the challenge of the interplay of ideas.

Though honest and far from glib, our politicians are not guileless, so use this parliamentary terms guide:

TERM: 'I withdraw.' TRANSLATION: 'My allegations are almost certainly true and will stick anyway, now that I've made them publicly, but since the Speaker is one of their party hacks not ours, I'll have to pretend to disavow them in order to get on to the more damning allegations of dishonesty and malpractice later on in my speech.'

TERM: 'That's not correct.' TRANSLATION: 'He's right, but by the time they've checked, the whole business will be forgotten.'

TERM: 'The minister is out of touch with his electorate.' TRANSLATION: 'My God he's a good minister—there must be some way of getting at him.'

TERM: 'I would require notice of that question.' TRANSLATION: 'I haven't the foggiest idea.'

TERM: 'The member is making debating points.' TRANSLATION: 'My God he's right.'

TERM: 'Ministers are constantly tripping round the world.' TRANSLATION: 'It's now long enough for them to have forgotten how many we had.'

TERM: 'A full and frank exchange of views with the American President.' TRANSLATION: 'I got my orders.'

TERM: 'Making a political football out of a complex issue.' TRANSLATION: 'They're on to a good thing.'

TERM: 'The people will not fall prey to glittering bribes.' TRANSLATION: 'We've not got much of a policy this time.'

TERM: 'I wouldn't stoop to deal with such tawdry accusations.' TRANSLATION: 'I couldn't.'

TERM: 'I don't want to use my full time.' TRANSLATION: "I shall only want a short extension.'

TERM: 'Despite their attempt to discover new policies the other side of the House haven't changed basically.' TRANSLATION: 'How come we've nothing new to throw at them.'

TERM: 'This is no time for defeatist talk.' TRANSLATION: 'We've got the country into a mess.'

TERM: 'That question does not follow from the first.' TRANSLATION: 'Good heavens, they forgot to brief me on that.'

TERM: 'I call on the Government to resign.' TRANLATION: 'I've run out of ammunition.'

TERM: 'The Opposition opposed the sale of state houses.' TRANSLATION: 'We've got to get them off the housing problem. They've got too strong a point.'

To change the subject from Parliament, as Mrs Kirk would say, we have a fourth stage of government, People's Democracy, though we should perhaps omit 'people's'—it worries Brigadier Gilbert, even with the P.D.S.A. Every third year, in November, power passes to you personally, though you may have to share it with up to one and a half million others, depending on how many bother to vote. Only now will you realise the full promise of New Zealand politics for they have the most promising politicians in the world. There is no corruption: they aren't the kind of politicians people would want to vote twice for. Besides, the New Zealander rarely puts cash down. Time payment is the system with politics as with cars. Win now, pay later.

Elections have little to do with politics. They are the local variant of that vital Pacific religious phenomenon, the Cargo Cult. Only in New Zealand does it reach the full apogee of its development. The cargo promised is more lavish and, instead of one prophet to promise it, the Kiwi can choose between three. Ministers who have been arguing the need for discipline, effort and restraint will suddenly discover that things have never been better. The country is moving to a limitless future given the continuation of present policies. Even Mr Muldoon will hover, momentarily, on the brink of a smile as his eyes move away from the television interviewer to seek out the camera. The Opposition, after three years of complaining about current messes and looming difficulties, will find that with a little painless correction administered by them, all will be well. Social Credit prophets, always inclined to inflation, will outbid both the others.

The rites are the same as in any other Pacific Island. The cargo is the same: cars (you will begin to feel like buying one), houses, cheap credit. You name it and if it's not against the moral code it's coming. Even if it is, the politicians will hold out imprecise hopes of a change in the code. Unfortunately, the electors only half-believe the promises. The age of faith died with Michael Joseph Savage, a political Liberace of his time. Now politicians have to promise ever more strenuously so they can combat disbelief.

Elections have occurred so regularly for so long that they are now firmly implanted on the collective subconsciousness. Like Pavlov's doggies, New Zealanders would still find themselves in orderly queues outside polling booths on the last Saturday in November every third year if Tom Pearce seized power and cancelled elections as a distraction from rugby. Kiwis abroad tramp alien streets looking for a polling booth because some deep tribal instinct stirs within them.

Kiwis vote for non-political reasons. Keep politics out of

elections. The N.Z.B.C. has already gone too far by calling in professors of political science to comment on the inaction like a Greek chorus which has wandered into a low class burlesque house by mistake. The scientists hover over the electorate like the Four Horsemen of the Apocalypse, only more portentously—and mercifully more briefly. They then return to their studies to carry out a detailed analysis which fails to emerge before the next election. They should stick to games-theory analyses of the New Zealand Rugby Union. New Zealand elections are the province of professors of anthropology and religious studies. They at least are trained to understand tribal ceremonies.

New Zealand political institutions are like any other local industry. The plant is small, outdated and orginally imported, though the rulers have tinkered with it, scrapping the Legislative Council packing room here, adding an Ombudsman machine there. Production is strictly for the home market. And it is heavily protected, otherwise Mr Lee Kuan Yew might take over and run the country on a part-time basis from his head office in Singapore. The real difference from similar industries overseas is the way the local staff, the 'politicians', run the plant.

Genus Politicus New Zealandiensis is not under flora so he must come under fauna. He is not a unique element in the local fauna, though the type is rapidly becoming extinct overseas, where it has been hunted down and pushed out by ruthless professionals. The British think of their politicians as an élite distinguished by ability and intellect. The Americans think of their politicians as corrupt; the honest politician is one who, when bought, stays bought. In New Zealand honesty is the norm, a testimony to lack of imagination and the unsaleability of the product rather than superior virtue. Politicians are essentially the ordinary bloke. The prime requirement is neither intellect nor ability but that of being (or appearing to be) a good bloke. In politics the good bloke syndrome finds its highest expression. The best politician is the one who blends most harmoniously into the Kiwi background.

In each party, selection of candidates is in the hands of party members who can be guaranteed to pick people like themselves. Like the selector, the candidate must live in the electorate so they'll know if he looks after his garden. He must have a wife whose looks and social poise won't make the homeliest selector feel threatened. Children and a dog are desirable for featuring on householder pamphlets and press publicity (in rural electorates add one more child and leave the dog off). He should preferably have attracted attention by his assiduous committee joining, by activity for appropriately wholesome causes, and by being seen at the R.S.A. He should display no hint of any abnormality in education, of superior intellect or peculiar sexual inclination. The unusual frightens New Zealanders; the like reassures them. They will seek it out and stick to it with determination. Abnormalities

should be disguised by frenzied housebuilding, concreting, or if possible, breaking-in of land. It is advisable to have had several jobs. This is known as valuable experience.*

* The situation is typified by one Social Credit candidate who told an eager *Press* reporter in 1969: 'As a man who during his life has worked on the railways and as a milk vendor, taxi driver, restaurant and pie-cart proprietor, he has come into contact with a great many people of all types . . . his grandfather was on the staff in Parliament Buildings.' Unfortunately this wealth of experience was put to the service of the wrong party. The candidate was heavily beaten.

Imagine the speech a locally born John F. Kennedy would have to make to get past the National Party selection meeting in Hawke's Bay:

'Ladies and Gentlemen. Since my family bought—er—settled in this electorate there have been wholly unfounded rumours that I am attempting to buy my way into politics. I give the lie to these allegations. Why have none of the allegators been man enough to come into the open? My father played as a child in the Karangahape Road. All he has he had to work hard for and he had to provide for a large family —in fact we could do with more of his kind of spirit—I sometimes think we're getting too dependent on the State to do things for us rather than doing them for ourselves.

'My father didn't believe in this new-fangled play-way stuff. He thought that sparing the rod was spoiling the child—and though I resented it at the time I think, looking back on it, he was right. At twelve I was walking barefoot behind the plough on one of—er—on the family farm. We were a large family so I had to go away to school, but at Christ's College District High School I was never one for book learning. Perhaps I spent too much time on the rugby field.

'Then my father had to go to England on business. Though I didn't want to go, at least it did show me how lucky we are in New Zealand. I can tell you, I couldn't get back quickly enough. As for my war service—well it's not something I often talk about. I had to lie about my age, I'm afraid, to get into the army, but I'll never forget the mates I made in those days and I'm sure my injuries haven't affected my ability to do my job in any way—in fact they've helped me to understand the meaning of suffering. It's something I hope we never have to go through again, but if we have to, we'll do our bit.

'I wasn't fortunate enough to marry one of our New Zealand girls. But my wife's learning our ways—she made her first scones last week and she's asked me to say that she hopes you'll drop in any time for a chat, just as soon as I've concreted the drive. When we're settled in our new palace—er—place, she'll be along to the Women's Division dressmaking circle.

'That's all I want to say. I'm not used to making speeches —and right now I'd sooner be out in the paddock. But then I sometimes think we've already got enough over-educated know-alls in politics. What we need is a bit more trust and integrity. Perhaps I'm a bit old-fashioned, but it's not a glib tongue that Hawke's Bay needs but someone with a stake in the electorate and who knows what it needs. And I hope you'll tell me.'

As a process of choosing, say, university staff, or directors of Dalgety Loan, this would be ridiculous. For choosing the men who decide on the fate of the universities and influence the destinies of Dalgety Loan, it is admirable. Politician is the only job in New Zealand for which neither qualifications nor training are necessary.

The job is essentially the same as that of the television frontman. In television someone else takes the decisions, decides the questions, arranges the discussion. The frontman only *seems* to be in charge.

So, in politics, the member of Parliament is a middle man. In power he explains, justifies and interprets the decisions of the public servants to the man in the street. In opposition he asks of the public servants the questions that the man in the street is interested in. Both jobs can best be done if the M.P. himself is either the man in the street or not long off it. Administrators need protective cover. It might as well be realistic.

Once elected, the honourable member (for he is always given the benefit of the doubt) has many interesting, although optional, things to do. The ugly, some of the unconcealably stupid, and those who have the misfortune not to get on with their party leader, become backbenchers. Their job is to speak. In Parliament they are reverse somnambulists, talking in other people's sleep. They discuss party preoccupations and the epoch-making concerns of their constituents: Mr May (at question time) —'When does the Railways Department intend to paint the Tawa station and overbridge which are at

present in a dilapidated condition?' Such a question allows Henry to sit back, confident that he can do no more to change the course of destiny, short of getting out his own paintbrush. The speeches continue (and are often repeated) outside Parliament, where M.Ps are expected to open fêtes (some of them worse than death), church bazaars, post offices, schools, annual general meetings and all those other things that Brian Edwards, Selwyn Toogood, or any other stray television celebrities are too busy to do.

The remainder of the M.Ps go on to higher things. New Zealand is an egalitarian community and anyone can get to the top; which is more of a threat than a promise. There are no formal requirements, though the constitution provides that National shall be led by a socialist and the Labour Party by a Tory. Neither the People's Walter nor the People's Norm can be deepest red, whatever they've done to the party's martyred dead (an obscure and somewhat tasteless reference to Arnold Nordmeyer, expelled from the Labour leadership when he was discovered to have a degree).

Outside these guidelines, there are no curbs to the full and happy life a minister can lead. Those who are out of hospital can travel or meet endless deputations. The minister's job carries with it immense dignity as well as someone more literate than himself to write his speeches. The one thing he must not do is to take decisions. These must be taken for him by his departmental officials and his party caucus. His job is to interpret one lot of these decision-makers to the other and defend both to the public. Like the backbencher he is a middleman, only he works wholesale rather than retail.

A minister also has the job of ritual soothsayer to the nation. The prime task of the politician in New Zealand is to tell the people what they want to hear. Not for him the stern imperatives of Churchillian oratory. He prefers the ritual incantation of platitudes, strung together by a stream of consciousness technique discovered well before James Joyce learnt how to write without fullstops. Richard John Seddon would stump the country telling each little community that it would have the roads, the bridges, the loans and the public works which in those simple days constituted happiness. Then he would move on to the next settlement to promise them exactly the same things. Those days are gone. The Press Association and the television now tell the whole country what is promised to each particular part. In any case, public taste has changed. Now we like slices of reassurance or pie in the sky. Policies, like butter, need spreading. So speechmaking becomes topdressing of platitudes, promises and reassurances.

Since the two last ones are in comparatively short supply, politicians have to pad them out and dilute them by energetically advocating policies which no one in his right mind would oppose. Politicians who can't tell the difference between the Apocrypha and the *New Zealand Woman's Weekly* compete to defend the Deity and the Christian religion against all sorts of dark threats. Time and energy are devoted to protecting wholesomeness, motherhood and the family, as though all three were threatened with overwhelming catastrophe from the New Zealand University Students' Association.

Like the Mafia, politicians work in a gang, a caucus nostra. Ever moderate, New Zealanders have compromised between the extremes of one-party and two-party systems which characterise less happy lands overseas. They have opted for a two-party system in which each party has the same policy. One party governs and the other opposes, both intermittently change round, and nothing happens. This is the real action, but there are all sorts of sideshows at the fair.

Moving, in the fashion of any good Labour man as he grows older, from left to right, let me begin with the Marxists. They owe more to Groucho than to Karl. New Zealand's communists have now split up into fifty-seven different varieties, which is two varieties more than the actual number of communists. In Dunedin, being closest to Russia, there lives a group of Marxists still as dedicated to Comrade Stalin as others in the town are to Bonnie Prince Charlie. There they sit perfectly preserved, like everyone else in that historical deep-freeze called Otago, in the attitudes of the 1930s. Further north, in Auckland, Comrade Mao is more fashionable. In-

deed the Communist Parties of China and New Zealand have issued at least one joint statement, a boost to the Chinese self-confidence which may have led directly to the Vietnam war.

There's no need to fear any of our resident concert party of communists as a revolutionary threat. In the first place, i.e. Auckland, they devote more time and effort to opposing each other than to subverting capitalism. In the second place, whatever energy and time they have left over is consumed by publishing pamphlets and periodicals which nobody reads and putting up election candidates that nobody votes for; demo-

cracy is the opium of the Marxists. Expenditure on election-
eering works out at over two dollars for every vote received.
At that rate they couldn't afford to win.

In any case Marxists are a small and dwindling band. The
increasing misery of the proletariat somehow doesn't apply in
a country where they are inconsiderate enough to buy more
cars and washing machines every year. The energies of the
young Left are going into the Progressive Youth Movement.
Yet a spectre will always remain to haunt us. If communism
did not exist the National Party would have to invent it.

Panning right, across the spectrum, brings us to a plethora
of mini-parties. Only inertia and laziness prevent New Zealand from developing as many parties as there are people.
It's as easy to form a party as to buy the *New Zealand Herald*
and twice as interesting. The number of parties contesting
the elections increases as the vote goes down. In 1969 puzzled
electors had to choose between fifteen parties with no Consumer Council to nominate a best buy. ('This candidate
wore out after eighteen speeches compared with an average
of eighty-two for others. We recommend him.')

There are also maxi-mini-parties. One such is the Country
Party, which intermittently makes an appearance. Country
parties come and go, the rut remains the same. In each case
the objective is to bring Downie Stewart back to power by
constitutional means. Liberal parties also flourish and die,
usually with policies of hanging, flogging, ending mollycod-
dling and other such liberal nostrums. The Constitutional
Society, also known as the political arm of the New Zealand
Who's Who, was long presided over by the late Sir Matthew
Oram, a former Speaker. Its traditional policy of restoring
the nineteenth century is little heeded.

Finally there are the provincial separatist movements. They
should by rights be strongest in Nelson which has been completely cut off from the rest of the South Island for twenty
years without anyone noticing. However, the National Government clearly exists only to persecute Nelson by abolishing
cotton mills, stopping railway building (Nelson has a notional
railway—something often described in other parts of the

country as a road) and other tortures. As a result all separatist passion in the province is channelled into the Labour Party. Otago is different. The Home Rule for Otago Movement would be very powerful, were it not for the fact that the *Otago Daily Times* (All the News that Fits, We Print) dare not back such a movement for fear of producing a Labour Provincial Council, with Mrs McMillan as first president and closing the *O.D.T.* as first policy.

This brings us to Social Credit, which campaigns to bring the pleasure of overdrafts to people without bank accounts. This theory of the continuous creation of credit was invented by an English engineer, Major Douglas. He omitted to patent his invention and though the Japanese didn't take it up, New Zealand did. The Social Credit Political League, present medium for the message, is more of a religious sect than a political party. It blends zeal for the crusade with a feeling of persecution, desire to illuminate mankind with a sense of alienation from it. In 1954 the league approached politics with all the charm and friendliness of Elliot Ness meeting the Mafia. Now it has compromised; the A : B theorem no longer plays on the Social Credit hit parade. About the only present use for the old economic doctrines is to provide the justification for lavish political promises. At election times Labour and National both go for the laxative image, promising to get New Zealand moving again (Labour, 1966) or to keep New Zealand on the move (National, 1969). Social Credit projects a positive deluge of benefits. It's also an ideal party for New Zealand, for overseas debt has made it a country run on hire purchase, a never-never land.

The league is happiest out of Parliament so that it need not take sides; the electorate has usually been happy to accept this interpretation of the league's best interest. Yet Mr Cracknell, an expert on ashtrays, was elected to represent the Northland Harbour Board for a three-year term. In this period he attended Parliament whenever he could get to Wellington and held his caucus meetings in the telephone booth in the lobby, though manifesting an unfortunate reluctance to be bound by caucus decisions. He was then ejected.

TAKE YOUR PICK

The good electors of Northland were voting not for him or his party but for a far higher and more noble cause: marginal seat status. Marginal seat status is provincial New Zealand's answer to the twentieth century. Inconsiderate economic forces pull development, industry and skills towards the larger centres of population (a euphemism for Auckland). So the provincial towns must vote marginal to keep up the supply of post offices, Government Life offices, coal-fired power stations, and airports. Northland's reward for its flirtation with Mr Cracknell was the most lavish programme of road building in the country.

Now for the big league: National, which runs the country, is led by Sir Keith Holyoake,* a Robert Menzies for beginners. The Labour Party is led by Norman Kirk, believed to be the

* Early in 1972 (when this book was far advanced in production), Jack Marshall, who had been taking over the Cabinet portfolio by portfolio, became leader, thus fulfilling the ancient prophecy that the meek shall inherit. As representative of the more reticent, retiring, thinking section of the party, Mr Muldoon became number two, thus paving the way towards a one-party State, for with Mr Muldoon standing behind Mr Marshall, who needs an Opposition?

largest Labour Party leader in the Southern Hemisphere. Opposition isn't a satisfying role, though the leader has almost as much power as Brian Edwards, so, to prevent the Labour Party members from becoming sullen, discouraged and disillusioned (or more so than usual), they are allowed to make the political running in the year and a half before the election and to carry all before them in the actual election campaign. Then, to set the balance right, the electors tramp out to the polls and keep National in power, preferably by as fine a majority as possible. This guarantees that the party won't dare to implement its policies. The election is usually a mere formality. The National Party pays for opinion polls so it knows the result in advance and judges its policy accordingly. When certain it is going to win (as in 1966) it will denounce all Labour's policies in advance of the poll and then implement them quietly afterwards. When more doubtful (as in 1969) it will go in for really bubonic plagiarism and either implement Labour policies in advance or include them in its manifesto.

This situation provides useful roles for almost everybody. The Labour Party is kept happy and busy exhausting itself in the continuous pursuit of new policies for National to steal, and in continuously renovating itself for a victory that isn't considerate enough to come. Of course Labour does from time to time hit on policies which National seems reluctant to steal. Labour then becomes so worried about this section of its manifesto that it is hardly mentioned. As for the Labour Party Youth Movement (also known as the Princes Street Branch or Dr Michael Bassett) it has a useful role in preaching the need for a policy relevant to the sixties, the seventies or whatever decade the party finds itself in. Finally, generations of political scientists can republish their 'Whither Labour?' articles at regular intervals.

From time to time even this surfeit of goodies is not enough. Then Divine Providence (Treasury code name for the I.M.F.) produces an economic crisis. Ministers cry, 'Do not adjust your government, the world is at fault,' but they look tired and say it lamely, so adversity stirs the electors into action and Labour comes to office. The party then incurs enough unpopularity in dealing with the crisis to guarantee that it remains in opposition for a further decade or two. This process (known as Nash's Law after the local reincarnation of a nineteenth century head of the British Treasury) was also popularised in Britain by Harold Wilson.

Every nation has its divine mystery, its central enigma. In Britain they puzzle over telling New Stork from Butter. Because New Zealanders are better educated and not allowed margarine they worry whether there is any difference between the political parties. Don't listen to the cynics. They may be the country's largest religious denomination but they are wrong. It is possible to tell the difference between Political Brand X and Brand XX. Both parties have policies. Both parties are honourable about implementing them—even when they would be better advised not to. Both parties behave differently because of conditioned reflexes. When things go well (that's election year) it doesn't really matter which party is in power. When things go badly (that's the year after the election) each party will choose different ways of getting at you for the over-spending they had encouraged you to go in for only a few months back.

You must first distinguish between Government and Opposition. This is easy because every member of a party team makes the same speech. The master speech is prepared by the party research officer who sits in a basement room in Parliament Building supplying speech notes to members.

Taking the Government members' omnipurpose speech first, the notes for this read:

1. Expression of pleasure at being in .... and recollection of excitement with which speaker first heard his great-aunt recount the details of her first (and only) visit in 1932.
2. Passing mention of deity-royal family—importance of family life, personal cleanliness and, if time allows, regular brushing of teeth.
3. Expression of faith in New Zealand's peculiar destiny, high standard of living and intrinsic ability of New Zealand people.
4. Need for tried and trusted leadership—and necessity of experience in face of looming problem of Common Market,

pollution, permissive society or long-haired larrikins depending on the I.Q. of the audience. Expression of confidence in
leader, possibly combined with statement that television does
not do him justice. Mention of Deputy Prime Minister. This
should not be too lavish lest it might anger Prime Minister
and indicate a taking of sides in a leadership struggle.

5. List of things Government will do and benefits to come
followed by refusal to buy votes and warning against promises
(easy, glittery or dazzling).

6. Increase in exports (change figures from volume to value
as circumstances require).

7. Rise in standard of living (quoting figures for cars, washing machines, fridges or Feltex carpets as necessary).

8. Increase in population—with discreet hint of Government
virility and heterosexuality.

9. Diffident voicing of doubts about loyalty, competence, asso-
ciates, and manliness of Opposition.

10. Quick mention of importance of environment and dangers
of pollution to show awareness of problem (rephrase if any
other problem becomes fashionable).

11. Quotation of statistics (seasonally corrected, base date
1957 for National, 1972 for Labour) proving that immigration
to Australia, cost of living, and infant mortality all increasing at slower rate than under previous governments.

12. Peroration expressing confidence in future if leadership
unchanged, rebuttal of unnamed critics of Prime Minister,
and praise of wisdom of New Zealand people in choosing
speaker and his party.

Government members can't be too critical and they cannot
claim credit for everything without being accused of immod-
esty. The Opposition has more latitude. The basic framework
of their speech, as prepared by their party research officer,
follows:

1. Expression of pleasure at being in .... and moving
recollection of help given to great uncle who passed through
there looking for work in 1932.

2. Concern about way in which standard of living and welfare
services in New Zealand are falling behind America, Australia,
Kuwait or Venezuela as appropriate.

3. Comparison of annual holidays, hours of work, overtime
rates in New Zealand with Scandinavia, America, Paraguay
or Uruguay as appropriate.

4. Expression of concern at increase in crime rate, gang rapes
and illegitimatcy, together with hint that Government is

either responsible in some unspecified fashion or soft in some unspecified way (or area). Need for law and order—with mention of good work done by police force in difficult circumstances.

5. Society, moral condition of, emphasis on decline and need for traditional values with much use of 'I may be old fashioned but', but without commitment to repealing legislation or any remedy beyond discipline in other people's homes.

6. Warning of dangers of complacency and emphasis on challenge of Common Market to prove need for new initiative and ideas.

7. Anxiety at slow growth rate despite energy, skill, competence, adaptability and drive of New Zealand people who deserve better leadership.

8. Quotation of statistics (weighted averages, base date 1949 for Labour, 1957 for National) to prove that immigration to Australia, cost of living, debt and infant mortality all at record levels.

9. Warning of deterioration of environment and growing threat of pollution with invocation of need for drastic action.

10. Prophecy of economic difficulties to come and troubled future if present unimaginative policies, tired leadership not changed.

11. Indication of way in which family allowances, G.M.S., sickness benefit and social security have all fallen behind cost of living, without commitment to definite sums for increase.

12. Peroration expressing confidence in native abilities of New Zealand people, listing benefits accruing from new welfare and economic policies and indicating painless solution to all problems under new leadership.

The whole science of statistics in New Zealand is, of course, devoted to comparing 1946-49 with 1950-57 and contrasting 1957-60 with 1961-72.

In the unlikely event of political change, these sets of notes can be simply swapped round.

It is necessary to keep the note of envy out of your voice when accusing opponents of fooling the people. Audiences over whose head the tide of figures normally flows without disturbing sleep might get restless if you compare output over two months of the new government with twenty years of the old. After a change, the Opposition must claim credit for all good as a continuation of trends set previously while

blaming everything else on perverse politics. The Government
can do the opposite. Each side can settle into its new routine.

You can now tell Government from Opposition. Next distinguish between Labour and National and you can follow
our endless permutations, for Labour in opposition is as different from Labour in power as National is from Labour. Go
to the party conferences. At National's, women wear hats,
earnest young men glasses, and older delegates have weather-
beaten faces and thornproof suits. The platform used to be
draped with the Union Jack, the better to disguise the party's
vigorous pursuit of the American alliance. Conversation between delegates will avoid politics and concentrate on stomach
troubles, heart complaints and other ailments until you're not
sure whether it's a party conference or an organ recital. At the
Labour conference there will be a smattering of beards and
long hair, a friendly chaos will prevail, and a succession of

young men will make challenging speeches on the need to win young voters, then disappear for ever having failed to secure immediate election to the National Executive since the qualifying age is sixty-five.

At branch level Nationalists are supposed to meet once a year. They rarely get together more often. Labour's are supposed to meet once a month. They manage once a year. Nationalists get a speaker on flower arrangement to discuss the Cabinet reshuffle. With Labour, the euchre report is more obsessive. Despite such powerful counter-attractions to television, both sides find it difficult to get a quorum. Those prepared to put up with the boredom in the hope of becoming High Commissioner to Australia are few.

Woe betide anyone who manages to overcome the insuperable difficulty of actually finding a party branch (for they are usually better concealed than communist cells). I remember my first Labour Party branch meeting in Dunedin and the extravagant welcome I got as the symptom of a revival of youthful interest, being the only person present under sixty. Two old ladies specially collected from Parkside Home to make a quorum regularly interjected, 'I'm seventy-nine you know' into our discussions—their sole contribution. My rise was rapid. At the first meeting I was elected delegate to the Labour Representation Committee. At the second, branch chairman. At the third, the young Mitchell was nominated to the City Council ticket. At the fourth, I was asked to go forward as the branch's nominee for the safe Labour seat in which we were the only form of Labour life still extant. At this point I left for England, not considering myself ready to take over the party leadership by attending a fifth meeting.

The same differences and similarities continue right up the party ladder. National, respected by many, and particularly themselves, as the party of efficiency, runs smoothly because it employs professionals to do the donkey work so the members can be free to prepare the supper. Labour shambles along by imposing an interminable burden of raffle selling which transforms members into walking Amplex advertisements, avoided by all but the unsuspecting. Paperwork also cuts down the time available for the really important discussions on how hard things were in the depression and how easy life is for young people. This latter conviction is shared by National Party branches, particularly in the country where branches are Federated Farmers meetings in another guise.

Macdonald's Law, named after a famous bowls player who succeeded for three decades in disguising the fact that the Labour Party National Executive had ceased to meet in 1940, states that politics is diluted in proportion to membership. The more members a party has, the more time is consumed on organisational matters, reports, remits and amendments. Thus the larger party is the happier. It is consumed with constant and completely apolitical activity, rather like the sorcerer's apprentice. This leaves the candidates and M.Ps free to get on with taking political decisions behind closed doors. As the law predicts, political activity is lowest in the National Party with over 200,000 members, higher in the Labour Party with 10,000, higher still in Social Credit.

A variation on Macdonald's Law is Wilson's Law of Political Altitude. Politics are diluted by altitude. Labour and National branches will both animatedly discuss the need to restore hanging, corporal punishment and firm discipline. Both will feel the welfare state encourages scroungers. Higher up the organisational ladder there is little time for such informed discussion. Organisational imperatives force politics out. Thus the Labour Party's New Zealand executive has no higher political thought than what time the tea and discuits will be served. Similarly, when asked in an interview why he had struggled to the top of the party pyramid, one Dominion president of the National Party replied, 'Because it is there'.

Now you must differentiate by policies. The Poms disguise basic greed as political philosophy; the Americans hire a public relations firm to paint it as pure altruism. Kiwi politicians are blunter, ever ready to call a spade a prohibited immigrant. 'Gimmee' is rarely presented as the advancement of welfare and the socially just society; 'Lemmee' only occasionally comes out as the need to stimulate the dynamics of competition. Compared with political debate overseas, both parties restrict themselves to the exchange of instinctive grunts, which is the reason why the ever tortuous English mistake New Zealand politics for dull.

First then the little clues. Both parties are political archaeologists constantly unearthing the past. Nationalists will talk about any, or all of the following:

1957 and £100 rebates.

1958 and Black Budgets and/or import restrictions, rationing controls, restrictions and shortages.

1943 and burnt ballot papers.

Danger of state ownership of all property.

Reminder that the other side opposed sales of state houses.

Iniquities of land sales control and possibility of restoration.

Threat of nationalisation of all business down to the corner dairy and suspicion that the recent (1932) dropping of the socialisation objective was insincere.

Labour men sling different ritual incantations back:

1967 or 1970 and mini-budgets.

Abolition of subsidies and free school milk with figures on increased incidence of rickets.

1957 and 25% rebates up to a maximum of $150.

1958 when the party attacked capitalisation of family benefit.

1938 when other side opposed social security ('organised lunacy').

1932 and responsibility for Depression. (This last is a concession to the slowly dwindling number of Labour men still running against the Coalition Government.)

Political debate like this will make the task of the future historian impossible, like an archaeologist reconstructing a civilisation on a site which has been progressively looted by bands of desperadoes (the politicians) and then picked over by coolies (the party researchers).

Policies spring from the class conflict of have-mores against have-lesses. Labour harps on education, social security, full employment and housing—things relevant to the preoccupations of what the Queen Mother would call 'the little people'.

National talks about farming, exports, and the American alliance, for they worship all things American, particularly dollars. They will claim that taxes have been reduced in 93 of the 74 years of National government, without explaining why you're paying more than you were five years ago.

After studying the New Zealand political scene, Chairman Mao evolved his theory of the pedant revolution because of the teachers—primary, postprimary and university—who man the Labour desks. The farmers confront them. Yet there are certain conventions of the constitution which insist that even in a National Government the Minister of Education shall be a teacher, if a presentable one is available, to show the portfolio isn't important. The Minister of Agriculture has to be a farmer to show that it is. The Minister of Finance has to be a man the people love to hate: an aloof, austere figure, waiting like an inverse Micawber for things to turn down. Collective hates can then be concentrated on him, so that the Prime Minister can get on with his real job of being loved. The least successful Finance Minister of modern times, Mr Lake, was so because he was too nice and cheerful and made people feel good and they went out and did dangerous things like spending money. On his death the government considered offering the job to Allen Klein on a commission basis. They eventually compromised on Mr Muldoon (R.21) because of the way his lip curled at the thought of freezes and squeezes. Just in case he should get those delusions of optimism, which have been known to overtake some Finance Ministers at election time, he is carefully watched over by the Monetary and Economic Council, liberally supplied with goats' entrails to warn of impending disasters. With its help Mr Muldoon has made a contribution to finance which can only be compared with that of Attila the Hun to Western civilisation.

Now you understand party differences, don't get obsessed by them. The fluctuations of the balance of payments and the state of livers at the I.M.F. have more impact on Kiwi lives than the hue of the government. You will be exhorted to cast an 'informed vote'. Read up on the candidates, their attitudes and backgrounds. Look at the history of the parties and the mail order catalogues they call manifestos. Then weigh up the policy and past performance of each party in the light of prevailing circumstances and the trends of the trade returns. Then boil all this information down into a choice of candidate. It's impossible. Even a computer couldn't do it—and it's not had anything to drink.

You've fallen into the trap of taking what New Zealanders say at face value. The exhorters of informed voting don't actually want you to think and investigate. They are merely anxious that you should vote the same way as they do. So walk into the polling booth and put yourself on automatic pilot. Your background will vote for you and if you try to vote against it you'll merely end up voting for Social Credit or some other lunatic, or doodling hysterical patterns on the ballot paper while sobbing convulsively.

Having voted, don't worry if your party doesn't get in. Governments are very generous, more generous to their opponents than their supporters. This must be so, because when National is in, the farmers grumble continuously; in Labour periods, the Federation of Labour drowns out every other pressure group with its complaints. You see, when Labour is in office it is anxious to prove itself respectable so it does what it thinks National would have done. National wants to be popular so it doesn't do what it really would like.

Also you must remember the basic characteristic of politicians: they are anxious to be loved. Katzengruber's Law of Political Psychosis states that the basic drive to enter politics comes from psychological insecurity. This can spring from many causes. Whatever the source of their anxiety, capitalise on it. Nothing frightens them more than the threat of withdrawal of love. Write to them threatening this and you will get long explanations. Write to the papers with the same threat and you'll get action. This is known as sensitivity to public opinion and it affects every institution of government. A fellow academic was once visiting the Governor of the Reserve Bank. In the centre of the gubernatorial desk, clipped, mounted and underlined, was a letter from that morning's paper making suggestions on banking policy. It was signed, 'Mother of Eight'.

Even if you don't particularly like the government, remember that governments only take decisions in times of economic crisis. They then impose import controls or remove them, impose taxes or slash subsidies, depending on how the mood takes them. These periods of frenzied decisions leave such a backlog of hostility that the government spends the rest of its term anxiously appealing for love. No more decisions are made. Instead the government assumes the role of ringmaster adjudicating between competing pressure groups and trying to hurt their feelings as little as possible.

The pressure group melées are the real substance of Kiwi politics. All the big things are settled—homes, jobs, the Blue Streak. So the real political arguments are now about the little things—for and against compulsory hydatids dosing, whether large-mouthed bass should be introduced into the rivers, how many toheroas can be dug up. Over these the pressure groups struggle.

Like beasts, pressure groups come in many shapes and sizes. Biggest and most fearsome are the throwbacks to prehistoric days, the monsters. The Federation of Labour, the Manufacturers, the Chambers of Commerce, and Federated Farmers (which also runs the agriculture portfolio through a front organisation called the Department of Agriculture). Not quite as big but compensating by making as much noise are bodies like the R.S.A. (motto: 'Make war not love') and the National Council of Women ('Make scones not love'). Some are minute, like the family planning movement ('Make love not children') and the Campaign for Nuclear Disarmament, which favours unilateral abandonment of New Zealand's massive nuclear stockpile. These are only random examples from the dense growth of pressure groups.

Pressure groups are intended to serve their members and give pleasures to their officers. These officials get a right to endless peregrination which keeps the skies black with pressure group officials ferrying from one conference centre to another. Without pressure group traffic N.A.C. could slim its services down to a De Havilland Moth plying monthly between Auckland and Wellington. Officials also get access to the great, though like ministers, the more they see of public servants the more they grow to talk and think like them.

Pressure groups pursue these goals in various ways. Where necessary they will fight each other, a process which serves no useful purpose but gives a great deal of pleasure. 'Federation of Labour unsympathetic to the needs of widow and orphan debenture holders', announces Associated Chambers of Commerce. 'Wharf workers near breadline,' wittily replies the Federation. 'New Zealand Federation of Sex Maniacs demands repeal of porn laws' may yet become a headline. In the 'good old days', which like any other immigrant you will find ended just before you arrived, pressure groups were led by giants who enjoyed nothing so much as wrestling in verbal mud. Sir Hamilton Mitchell, A. P. O'Shea and F. P. Walsh were always good for a quote. Once when I interviewed Walsh he demanded to know whether I was 'a Roman' (candle presumably) before the interview began. He then went on to denounce opponents who had risen 'from bogs to riches'. For some reason this was not in the final broadcast. In any case, though Hamilton Mitchell soldiers on, the giants have really been replaced by the blandness of the professional public relations men.

When not fighting, pressure groups can form coalitions. 'Our members not getting a fair crack of the whip,' say N.Z. Sadists' Society and N.Z. Masochists' Association in a joint demand for increased import quotas for instant whip. Most important of all, pressure groups have to cajole ministers. All have equal rights to earbash members of Cabinet. The Government, for its part, is anxious to co-operate. To go against any pressure group is to court a storm of protest and unpopularity. Ministers have therefore attempted the taming of the shrewd by keeping all the groups happy. Faced with problems, overseas governments take decisions. The New Zealand rulers call a conference of pressure groups:

1941 Stabilisation Conference
1960 Industrial Development Conference
1963 Export Promotion Conference
1964 Agricultural Production Conference
1968 National Development Conference
1984 Conference Promotion Conference.

As this technique is perfected and a higher standard of living provides more cake to share out, one can glimpse the ultimate system of non-government which will be perfected. Already all difficult decisions on road-building and spending have been handed over to the National Roads Board. More and more areas can be handed over in the same fashion. Finally, divested of all its responsibilities, the government can concentrate all its undistracted energies on its main concern and its most difficult job—being loved. The Kiwi art of politics will have reached its ultimate development: politics will have been completely excluded from politics.

SEX
or the New Zealand
Woman's Weekly

MOST COUNTRIES have oppressed minorities. New Zealand has an oppressed near majority, sometimes called The New Zealand Woman, sometimes known by her Christian name, Sheila. She's constructed locally from internationally approved patterns. Basic design is good and sturdy, though finish is unimaginative and trimmings limited. Controls are in the usual place and she needs little attention or maintenance: mumble at her occasionally, slap her on the back (never the bottom) and you can ignore her for hours. Above all, she's clean—fanatically so—and you will be, too, if you have anything to do with her. Yet aside from her outstanding contribution to the soap industry, what is her role? America is female dominated; France is male dominated. New Zealand you have to accept as a world divided into 'his' and 'hers'.

The 'his' compartment includes all the positions of power and the interesting jobs, all the folk heroes and all the dominant myths: sport, war and virility. Woman's role is to run the home, raise the children and make the scones. Like Dr Johnson, a Kiwi is 'better pleased when he has a good dinner upon his table than when his wife talks Greek', though

he might tolerate a little flower arranging. Naturally the Outward Bound Trust, considering courses for girls, thought
flower arrangement, make-up and nursing more appropriate
than the more energetic pursuits for boys. With the comfort-
able average measurements of 36-28-39, Norma Average is
built to be mater not Mata Hari.

Despite her impressive statistics, Women's Liberationists
find the Kiwi woman as underdeveloped as Twiggy. She leaves
school almost a year before the male and she's half as likely
to go to university. New Zealanders are low on the world
league for the proportion of women working. Only a third go
out to work and then usually in lowly paid jobs: a seventh
of men workers get under $1,400 compared with two-thirds of
women, while the average man gets over $1,000 a year more
than the average woman. Female Cabinet Ministers are as
rare as the captive kakapo, no woman has ever run a government department, only eleven have ever sat in Parliament,
and now only 5 per cent of M.Ps, 7 per cent of those embalmed in *Who's Who* and 8 per cent of doctors are believed
to be female. The rare woman who gets to the top gets there
by transforming herself into a man in skirts, an embattled suf-
fragette, or as a token gesture—most bodies feel it necessary
to appoint a woman, an advisory broad, in the same way as a
token Maori. Even the leaders of the campaign for female
emancipation are men. Like its counterparts elsewhere, the
Pohutamanurewa Women's Liberation Movement (membership three) has a male quorum after 9.30 p.m.—the two
women members have to be home early to prepare hubby's
supper and bake cakes.

A situation which horrifies overseas emancipationists hardly
interests the New Zealand woman. She's programmed to want
something different. Unimportant, honorific positions from
Prime Minister to chairman of U.E.B. can be left to mere
males. The female has real power and a more fulfilling role.
The male clings to the myths of dogged masculinity as social
conformity, and the growth of organisations and bureaucracies steadily emasculate him. The New Zealand woman is
still a pioneer, the last to savour the joys of being an inde-

pendent small businessman. She commands and manages the home unit. She determines the destinies of its denizens, mobilises its resources, manages its labour force of husband and children. Welfare and tax determine the floors and ceilings of the man's income. Much more important in determining the family's welfare is the way the woman mobilises the minimum the husband provides. Her housekeeping, budgeting, scrimping and saving and her efforts at the cottage industries of dressmaking and bottling make all the difference to the family's wellbeing.

The Kiwibird has the job of the small entrepreneur or the pioneer. She also has the characteristics. No wilting violet she, with her capacity for hard work and her dogged toughness. The dull plumage hides a fierce spirit. She knows what she wants—a husband, a lovely home, children, preferably though not necessarily in that order. Woe betide anything or anyone who stands in her way for she's a fierce and terrifying species. Her looks betray her spirit. Where the Kiwi male has a face younger than his body, her efforts have told to such an extent that her body is younger than her face.

Unfortunately her role doesn't provide universal satisfaction. Since she marries at 20 and has produced 2.6 children by the time she's 28, the joys of being a homemaker (notice the distinction from the English 'housewife') can pall when the children grow up, if only because it's useless. Sometimes she takes refuge in neurotic symptoms from backache to the National Council of Women. Or she throws herself into a strident hostility to change because she feels herself let down and without realising why, dimly puts it down to forces beyond her control. More than one in three go back to work around forty as an under-paid labour force, though slightly less exploited than the remainder, who devote themselves to the frenzied organisational work which alone keeps the machinery of welfare and education going. Committees are the opium of the people. The field of endeavour ranges from the Women's Division to the Mothers' Union competition for the best pikelet. Rarely does the embattled female fighting the rearguard action of life on one or all of these fronts realise that she is doing all this because the role she is programmed for has let her down.

Compared with the dogged singlemindedness of the single ladybird, and the implacability of the Great New Zealand Mum, the man's role is that of an ephemeral fainéant. While she bottles, he gets pickled, seeking escape from a home he can't dominate, in the boozy camaraderie of the pub or the solitudes of the garden. The only thing he's allowed to run is the car. He hasn't even got the initiative to form the Men's Liberation Front, the Y Front, to support his case.

While other advanced countries move towards unisex, this role tension between men and women is a basic division in their society. In literature it becomes a dominant theme of intermittent guerilla war or entrenched mutual incomprehension. In life it is the weak spot of their paradise, a vague, little understood dissatisfaction, a weakness in the roles they think should satisfy and fulfil, but somehow don't. In other countries the social battleground reflects the basic tension in society: in Britain, class; in America, colour. In New Zealand the battlefield is sex.

Your first impression will be that sex does not exist. The word is not used and the act itself is referred to as UNO, as in the phrase, 'They were going out with each other for six

months and (pause) you know'. UNO is thus different from 'yer know', because the one is something too shocking to talk about, the other too boring to discuss. Yet even when you know the name it is difficult to discover whether UNO exists. It may have been abolished as a distraction from the war effort by a government committed to the socialisation of the means of reproduction, distribution and exchange.

Where America goes topless, New Zealand has pioneered topdressing. The porn laws protect New Zealanders against the imminent threat of invasion from Denmark. No electrode-loaded volunteers devote themselves to a labour of love in the back seat of a mock-up car in some Auckland University laboratory and *Patterns of Sexuality in a Northland Town* by those well known social eroticians and bicycle menders Fischbein and Roganblatt remains unwritten. In Britain, women's magazines devote themselves to the sexual problems of their readers: the formula for a successful newspaper's women's page is ritual doses of abortion, illegitimacy, divorce and the pill. New Zealand counterparts tackle more fundamental problems: 'What to do about my winter sweet shrub which is making no growth, while the leaves have become brown. P.F. Auckland'. The Havelock you will hear about is North not Ellis and it is not necessary to get *New Zealand Wildlife* under plain cover.

Compared with Britain, this looks to be a cautiously antiseptic society. Prostitutes are as common as coelacanths and in most places taxi drivers will ask *you* where *they* can get a woman. Nary a nipple will confront you from the newspapers. Two-thirds of the population has fluoride in its water (the rest oppose it nail if not tooth) and you may well conclude that fluoridation eliminated nipples with dental caries. The idea of key parties where wives are swapped by the throwing in of car keys is unthinkable in a society more likely to throw in wives and swap precious cars.

Then you will begin to notice symptoms of UNO. In pub and rugby club, beer inflates the imagination, if not the libido. Men are men and women grateful for it—often. The Homeric narrators become the Edmund Hillarys of sexology;

life a kind of sexual Outward Bound course. No scientific accuracy exists because Kelburn harbours no Kinsey defining norms for Ngaio or frequencies for Feilding. Yet feats are recounted in action replays, feats which would have tested the stamina of a sex-crazed superman, raised on vitamin E in Nero's Rome. The narrators may exaggerate slightly in their surveys of the performing arts, but at least they think about sex.

Then you notice another symptom: the titivation industry. Much of this is imported. They don't assemble pornography locally under licentiousness and the Feltex version of *The Carpetbaggers* has yet to be filmed, so the pornshop is not the grossest part of the G.N.P. as in Scandinavia. Nevertheless, the sex substitutes are there. Look at the movie billings. One newspaper described *Irma La Douce* as 'a story of passion,

bloodshed, desire and death—in fact everything that makes
life worth living'. Others follow on similar lines. 'Insatiably,
music drove her onward'—*The Sound of Music*. 'Shocking
things, things that astonished the world, happened in this
car'—*Chitty, Chitty, Bang, Bang*. *Truth* titivates. Its bill-
boards are usually more exciting than the actual newspaper,
but its headlines also excite. 'Bedding-out in the North
Island'—gardening column. 'The Master and the Forty Boys'
—overcrowding in primary schools. Here is a nation sub-
limating.

Stage three of the process of adjustment is the assumption
that beneath the surface New Zealand throbs with a sexual
activity from which you alone are excluded. You see few outward symptoms simply because sex is the most asexual activity. Everyone is sexually content, possibly exhausted. The
prostitute has vanished because no one needs her. You alone
are not getting your share and you begin to feel like the
psychiatrist who wanted to be a sex maniac but failed the
practicals.

Understanding comes as a compromise between these
extreme views of bromideland or wall to wall sex. As in everything else, they conform to a norm: a quarter-acre, one-car,
three-children, two-orgasm family. UNO exists. Unfortunately
it can't be talked about. This is partly because of their puritan legacy which makes it easier to get sex than actually
discuss it. The small town environment, when Big Neighbour
tenderly watches over them every step every yard of the way,
also makes frankness difficult. Note that in Britain, adverts
for feminine deodorants are quite explicit on where and why
they are to be applied. Counterpart adverts in New Zealand
could be for catarrh.

UNO involves relationships between people, deep feelings
and emotions, things the New Zealander has been conditioned
to avoid and repress. It brings up basic problems of the relationship between the sexes, that fault line in the New Zealand
society. In America the social battleground is the streets—in
New Zealand it is the bedroom. Here the role conflicts and
tensions which characterise this society are put to the basic

test. The battle goes on in an atmosphere of sullen incomprehension. They don't know what it's all about.

Hence the embarrassed silence: the altar of hymen has to be discreetly draped in candlewick. Children have to be left to find out for themselves which, being good Kiwi pragmatists, they promptly do. This is perfectly acceptable. UNO itself isn't objected to—just indications that it goes on. A deaf ear is turned to anything that goes bump in the night, but one mistake brings the shotguns out and makes the erring youngsters sooner wed than dead.

If anything becomes public, the government will appoint a Royal Commission or the Railways Department will inquire into the Bluff-Invercargill train. This is the morality of 'thou shalt not be known to' rather than 'thou shalt not'. Negative

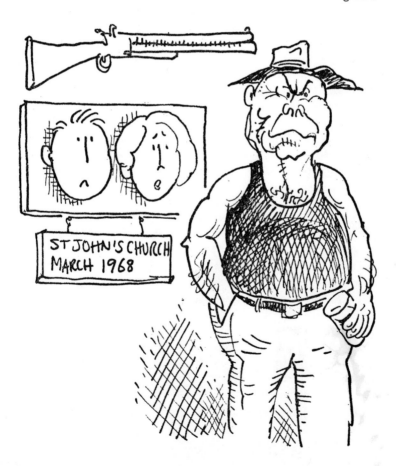

all this may be, but it's vigorous. Since it can't stop intercourse, it will stamp out contraception. It can't check conception, so it will prohibit abortion. Critics who attack such
acts as making bed situations worse, completely mistake the
importance of morality, which isn't really about other people
but about salving our own consciences. The job of the moralist is really to push the inconsiderate tip of the iceberg (the
point at issue) back under the water.

Formal instruction is ruled out, by their religious belief in
the trinity of monkeys, so the great amateur tradition takes
over. After a collective initiation in the group gropes, which
pass for teenage parties, the explorers are off on their own
('together we found out'). Their endeavours are confined to
cars, fields and livingroom floors, so as to reinforce the inbuilt
feeling that sex is dirty and beastly, and to preserve the feeling that marriage and clean sheets are a desirable goal. New
Zealanders are among the highest users of the pill in the
world (indeed thanks to it there will be over a quarter of a
million fewer New Zealanders by 1990 than there would
otherwise have been). Yet it is officially denied to the unmarried, which explains why the number of babies born in the
first seven months after marriage now runs at around a third
of nuptial first births and why the illegitimacy rate is second
only to Sweden and has been rising more rapidly than practi-
cally any country, even without encouragement from the

Monetary and Economic Council. Progressive churchmen have long been considering changing the marriage service to read, 'I did'. Small wonder that in 1969 the government 'authorised further research into the causes of the increase in extramarital intercourse', a study which would have been as enjoyable as it was pointless.

So there's your final picture. New Zealand is a society in which sex undoubtedly exists—in fact it's almost as common as rugby and can produce just as many injuries. Yet like rugby, it has to be restricted to amateurs. There is no pulsating promiscuity, just a rather sad amateur experimentation, a low standard of loving. In a drugged sleep, William James once thought he had stumbled on the key to the human dilemma. Hastily he wrote it down. He awoke next morning to read the legend, 'Higamus hogamus, woman is monogamous. Hogamus, higamus, man is polygamous'. His disappointment was not at the triteness of the message but because it did not really apply to New Zealand. Big Neighbour behind the venetian blinds does not allow the male Kiwi to be anything more than monogamous. His fierce female mate is determined to be nothing else. The unmarried experimenters enjoy a monogamy before marriage that's almost as glum as the monogamy after marriage; by the time they are married they have lost the taste for the whole business.

In America they escape from monogamy by adultery; in New Zealand they escape by segregation, hence their parties. These typically fall into two camps: an unbeleaguered garrison of women and the men clustering in the kitchen to keep supply lines short. This enables men to talk about ephemera like sport, cars and sex and women to talk about homes and children. Their concerns are always the more basic and practical.

The New Zealand marriage is the transfer of the embattled sexual relationship from car seat to candlewick. The system isn't likely to change. Co-education doesn't undermine the set-up for it makes the Purdah Principle informal rather than formal. Even emancipation will work against women unless it is total and complete. For a woman going out to work means letting go of the tiller and surrendering real power for a dull job and a low wage. Even the extra income only boosts the man's spending power since the Kiwi-hen is constitutionally incapable of spending money.

As for UNO it can only flourish when removed from the battleground and Big Neighbour. Visiting sailors, pop groups and American forces in war and what passes for peace are all outside the integration machinery so they find our sex life like our welfare state: rough and ready but free.

Still, I don't want to seem too critical. The New Zealand woman is the most attractive in the world. She's the best housekeeper and she brings up the cleanest children in conditions so antiseptic Dr Barnard would be proud to operate in them. She may prefer Alison Holst style to Graham Kerr but her cooking is certain to win your heart. It was after all Dr Barnard who remarked that the best way to a man's heart is through his stomach. And even if she weren't quite as good as I'm painting her I'd never dare tell you. She might break my arm.

SEVEN DAYS SHALT THOU LABOUR: The Games Kiwis Play

NEW ZEALAND is a land without leisure. What you call leisure time, Kiwis know as a period of maximum exertion. Outside working hours this is an ant hill (as distinct from Cashmere, the aunt hill) of effort. Inside working hours they recover. Maximum ingenuity has to be exercised in spreading out formal 'work' and reducing its strain to conserve energy for the ordeal ahead. The moralist may complain about lazy and slipshod workers. No one heeds him. The forty-hour week is a necessary recovery period for the other 128. Unlike the Germans and Japanese, New Zealanders have a sense of priorities. If they work hard it must be for themselves.

Leisure is so exhausting because there is nothing to do. Other countries have leisure and entertainment industries. Bowling alleys, drive-in brothels, theatres, clubs and other institutions cater for every taste from black currant cordial to geisha. Everything is done for them, so the workers can gallop back to their factories relaxed, refreshed and entertained.

In New Zealand it's different. Show biz hardly exists outside of a few itinerant pop groups, the Rev. Bob Lowe and that popular group, Dr Geering and the Presbyterian General Assembly. Visits from overseas artists like LBJ are few and expensive. By the time they get there they're not at their best after an exhausting trip. Lord Reith, a titled undertaker who believed that television was a branch of the embalming industry, still wanders N.Z.B.C. corridors, giving people what is good for them rather than what they want. As for night life, cities, while beautifully planned, are so well laid out that you wonder how long they've been dead. A search for the liveliest spot in town usually ends up at the Y.M.C.A. As for discotheques, in the world of the with-it they stand without, though a few daring entrepreneurs have converted their milkbars into psychodelicatessens. Ten o'clock closing has hardly made the pubs social centres; in mixed bars you have to ask for an estimate before you drink.

Restaurants are poor by overseas standards. When Graham Kerr talked of 'New Zealand, Land of Food', pies may have entered his mind but he was probably thinking of sandwiches. This is their basic food as well as the foundation of their way of life. Before the sandwich all men are equal. It sustains more people more cheaply to the ton than any known nutrient, even Asia's rice. It allows Kiwis to spend their money on essentials—such as cars and slimming cures. Schoolgirls stoke up on it into unlovely monsters beyond the help of power net Lycra or Maidenform bra. The menfolk are de-energised by the cloying pap. Citizens only eat out when they've got sandwiches. Otherwise it's too expensive. With a night out costing as much as a gnome for the garden there's really no choice. After a day of indigestion the meal is forgotten. A gnome is forever.

The Kiwis entertain themselves. Leisure begins at home. In the day they entertain there with coffee, at night with beer, and if the furniture needs renewing they give a party, pronounced with a 'd' to distinguish it from the less important political version. Whatever the social class of the host, parties are all eatathons and drinkathons. If it's a student do, keep your half-G up your jumper. If everyone is wearing suits it might be a mistake to paw your host's wife too soon. If it's your party insure against damage, though remember third party rates are high. Attempting to ingratiate myself with my students, I gave occasional parties while my house lasted. At the penultimate party the bed legs were broken off by the weight of couples dancing on it (this was, after all, New Zealand). At my final party, a fellow lecturer was pushed through the livingroom window and a gatecrasher locked himself in the lavatory for four hours, with disastrous consequences for the lawn.

If you are at a loose end ring a taxi firm and ask them to drive you where the action's thickest. Or follow people home from the pub and sidle in with them. Or join the other cars prowling the streets looking for signs of life. You won't be welcome but it would infringe traditional hospitality rituals to throw you out before you actually collapse vomiting on the carpet. After all, the party is the great Kiwi contribution to social betterment. One of the great literary classics is called *Government By Party*.

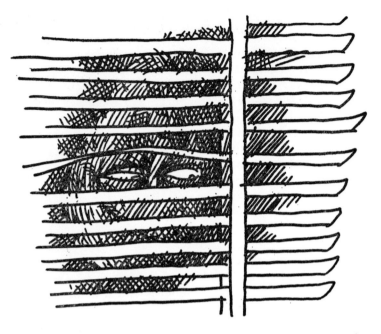

The home is the focus of the nation's life. Other countries go out for entertainment—Englishmen to sit in pubs, Ulstermen to murder each other in the streets. Kiwi homes are so much bigger, better and more beautiful, veritable people's palaces, that the occupants don't want to leave. The homes are also so expensive they can't afford to. The home is the venue for their most popular forms of entertainment: television, gardening and peering out of the window. It's also a hobby you inhabit, and so exhausting that no New Zealander ever calls his house 'Mon Repos'.

Americans flee the noisy cities to the quiet of suburbia. If you want weekend peace you must go to town. The suburbs are a cacophony of power drills, motor mowers, hammers, carpet and child beating and revving cars, all punctuated by the screams of amateur roof menders falling to their deaths. A New Zealand house begins life as a 1,000-square-foot wood or brick box, sitting in a sea of mud and rubble rather like Passchendaele. Within months the garden is a condensed and improved version of Versailles, likely to turn Capability Brown green with envy. Hand-manicured lawns get more care and attention than the owner's hair. Vegetable gardens carry a crop large enough to feed the entire Vietcong for decades.

The house's turn comes next. First a decoration, then an extension and enlargement, then an extension and enlargement to the extensions and enlargements. Once the major work is done, maintenance, redecoration and the addition of the occasional bedroom or ballroom keep things going until it's time to move on and begin over again. The Englishman's home is his castle. It's the New Zealander's mistress.

All this he does himself. In countries where work is highly specialised, do-it-yourself is a kind of escape from specialisation of labour, a return to craftsman traditions. The man who spends his life on a car conveyor belt tightening, or in Britain half-tightening, the fourth fender junction bolt can recapture the joy of being a jack of all trades. In New Zealand work isn't specialised. The only division of labour is the relationship between Tom Skinner and Norman Kirk. It is a nation of all-rounders who have to repair cars, build houses or decorate them because no one else will do it for them. Break down by the roadside and any passing driver can repair your car; one astute Englishman took a wreck from the scrapyard, dumped it by a country road, and by the time the twentieth passing driver had contributed his skills he had a machine capable of 0-60 in 10 seconds and 58.5 m.p.g.

I still remember the hysterical laughter on the other end of the line when I rang a Dunedin plumber to ask him to put a washer on the tap. My inability at gardening was a short-lived joke until the landlord realised that the psychosis was incurable. Then it became a subject for hostile comments and surreptitious dawn visits to do the garden with muffled mower while I slept. I was lucky. One friend allowed his garden to get into such a state of neglect that the neighbours

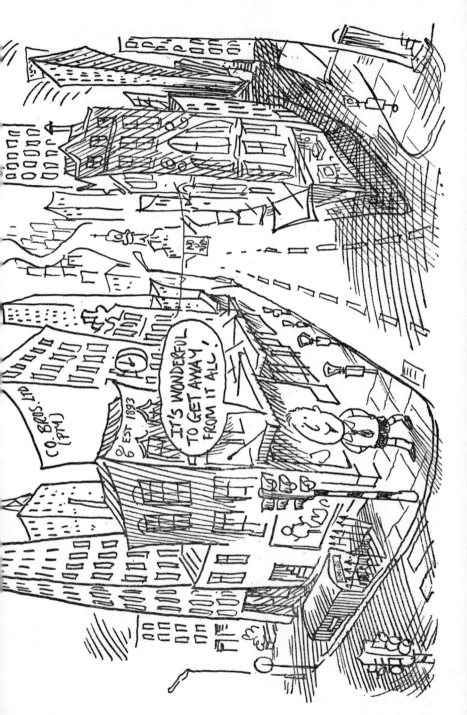

reported him to the Health Department, presumably after finding the Security Service reluctant to intervene. No official inspection machinery is necessary when Big Neighbour watches, and most New Zealanders spend Sunday afternoons driving round the suburbs inspecting everyone else's homes and gardens. The law intervenes but rarely, as when Otago University students started an epidemic of gnome stealing and butterfly daubing. This ended only when Mrs McMillan threatened to reintroduce the death penalty.

The home is a basic unit of production for children and goods. Other countries have mass production and conveyor belts. New Zealand needs cottage industry because it is less efficient. For the men the home is a garage and service station. The car isn't a consumer durable but a shrine, as well as being one of the few means of population control not proscribed by the Pope. For it kills over six hundred people a year. There is one car to three people because home garages keep on the road cars which would elsewhere appear only for veterans' rallies. It is a bit early to tell, but New Zealand may have discovered the secret of perpetual motion. The glory that was grease.

The home is also a market garden. And a brewery. The massive hoardings which proclaim 'Dominion Bitter' aren't to encourage you to drink this brew, but to express the feelings of the directors about their untaxed competitors.

The female production staff devote themselves to making jam, clothes, cakes and scones on a massive scale. The fruit is better preserved than the women. In the preserving season places where teenagers meet are suddenly all male—the girls are bottling. 'She's a bottler' is the highest praise a man can give about a woman. Yet female ingenuity extends in all directions. The *Woman's Weekly* regularly offers thousands of ideas for economy, ranging from making candlesticks out of bobbins to interuterine devices out of short ends of fencing wire. Indeed its surprising that dustbin men have to call at most New Zealand homes. Continuous recreation of matter was invented here.

This massive cottage industry allows the people to afford

all the consumer durables they couldn't buy if they had to spend money on clothes, vegetables or jam. Unfortunately it also makes these things inordinately expensive for the less dextrous.

Most people are exhausted by the demands of their homes and leave them only to rest and recuperate. Yet for those of insatiable energy there is a range of do-it-yourself activity outside. Elsewhere some act, sing or play, others pay to see them. In New Zealand everyone has the right to sing in grand opera, dance classical ballet or play in the symphony orchestra. Unfortunately all too many of them do.

Voluntary effort runs the political parties, and helps educate the children. Volunteers also provide nursery education, many of the welfare services and much of local government. Political scientists equate a country's degree of democracy with the vigour of voluntary organisations. New Zealanders are among the most enthusiastic joiners in the world. If wife swapping or sex orgies did catch on, they would form committees to organise them. The purpose of an organisation is usually irrelevant. It exists mainly to provide an outlet for energy, bring people together, and keep them off the streets.

Committees also organise sports. Tom Pearce's Law states that one hundred full-throated spectators and ten organisers, officials and administrators are necessary to put one man on the rugby field, a bigger back-up than the American army has hors de combat. Old rugby players never die, they graduate to committees. Study of the labyrinthine processes and the inscrutable personalities of the New Zealand Rugby Union is the Kiwi counterpart of the C.I.A. science of Kremlinology.

Sport isn't merely a physical expression of do-it-yourself. New Zealanders aren't a peaceful people and if they can't fight German enemies or thump American allies they need aggressive sport as an outlet for their violent instincts. War and sport bring out the beast in them. Yet sport is the cause of the country's social progress. Would the social security system have come into being without the incentive of the 20,000 injuries a year inflicted on the rugby field? Sport is also a major political issue. Look at the energy expended in

keeping politics out of sport or Maoris out of South Africa or South Africans out of New Zealand. Look at the interruption of parliamentary debates to announce results, or at the meteoric rise of one Minister who threatened to resign from Parliament if his local trotting club didn't get extra racing days. Sportsmen are the folk heroes. If they could manage words of more than one syllable they would be the nation's leaders too. Sport is a vital element of colour and excitement in the people's lives. In short it is their religion.

This doesn't mean they are all sportsmen. A 1966 survey of leisure time showed that two-thirds of those interviewed played no sport and a fifth took no interest, but these are

lower proportions than any other country and the same survey showed that a third of the men devoted five hours or
more to sport each week. New Zealand has more sporting
opportunities. Britain boasts 64 racecourses for 50 million
people and as many universities. New Zealand has only seven
universities but 80 racing clubs and 30 trotting clubs. It crams
271 licensed racing days and 133 trotting days into a 365-day
calendar.

To succeed, Kiwis concentrate their energies on a limited
range of sports. The girls concentrate on hockey and netball.
Men play rugby and cricket. Swimming, soccer and rugby
league are also permitted. One of them you must be good at
or at least interested in if you are to avoid ostracism; Lord
Rutherford wasn't good enough to be an All Black so the only
future for him was to go overseas and split the atom.

Sport is the only field where professionalism and skill are
tolerated. Kiwis excel at rugby because their children are
drilled from an early age, adolescents inspired with a lust to
kill which makes the Kamakaze pilots of World War II look
like simpering girls. A couple of games after their arrival, a
French rugby team had suffered two sprained ankles, two back
injuries, two hamstring injuries, one scalp wound and one
burst blood vessel. Harder grounds were not wholly to blame.
Also New Zealand had the wisdom to concentrate on a game
which only four other countries play, and they only as one
game among several. Thus New Zealand is able to lead the
world, with the possible exception of one of the four other
countries. Finally there is no international market in rugby
thugs. A ballet dancer would go overseas to reach his peak.
The rugby player's art reaches its finest expression in his
homeland.

Every so often New Zealand sends overseas as ambassadors
the All Black team, much as if Haiti sought to win the
world's esteem by sending the Tonton Macoutes as pleni-
potentiaries. Internally all is dedication. Tom Pearce was not
being too flowery when he once exhorted the nation: 'Now
that this team of very fine New Zealanders is about to leave
these shores it is incumbent on every loyal New Zealander to

get wholeheartedly behind the team.' It could be painful to get in front, but unless you take an interest there'll be nothing else to talk about for the next few months. Courteous New Zealand husbands have been known to ask their wives if there was anything they would like to declare before the tour commenced and family talk ended.

As a final pastime, the New Zealander has the great outdoors, greater and more extensive than anywhere else. The coastline divides up at three feet and eighteen sandflies per inhabitant, so a crowded beach is one on which you can see people. Hong Kong has 243 vehicles to every mile of road, New Zealand roads work out at over a hundred yards per car, enough even for me to park. The mountains are one per active climber. The whole country could be shared out at 27 people per square mile compared with a jostling 577 in Britain. Every year 500 tons of fish are pulled out of Lake Taupo alone and 100,000 deer and several hunters are riddled with lead. Indeed, old-timers will tell you that you were safer on Vimy Ridge than in some of the New Zealand forests. Tramping tracks like the trail to Milford take a harder pounding than any parade ground. Pity any foe with the temerity to invade New Zealand. The whole population would simply take to the hills. Guerilla war would decimate the entire Red Chinese Army in days.

The outdoors is normally reserved for holidays. You will recognise them because activity rises to ever more frenzied levels. In Britain holidays are an escape from reality, two hectic weeks on a package tour to a world which is slowly being plasticised, processed and sanitised for trippers. With the Kiwi, they are a concentration of reality, a period in which the people leave their houses and go to camping sites or motels, where life can go on as normal, the women cooking, the men tinkering. Holidays New Zealand style can also mean visiting relatives or friends and living off them. The country is a vast network of obligations and owed visits. Not even Petone is immune. When people with sleeping bags arrive at your door talking of a chance encounter in the Midland Hotel five years before, or a distant relationship with your wife's mother's first cousin, to turn them away is a breach of hospitality. So is taking seriously their offer to sleep on the floor. They want a bed, yours if necessary. No New Zealander away from home ever goes short of a bed, though as a Pom you may well be too squeamish to exploit a system which demands only thousands of relatives and brazen insensitivity.

Perhaps all that I've described, the do it yourself world of industry, entertainment and holidays, seems a little crude and unsophisticated to you. You may miss excellence and expertise. Seriously, though, life is better. You'll be doing things for yourself. After the initial blunders you'll come to enjoy it. If you don't you can always go back home and pay someone else to do everything for you. Even grumbling.

THE KIWI SNIGGERS: A Brief Guide to New Zealand Humour

THE MEDIUM
is the TEDIUM

MOST COUNTRIES have some pastor of souls tenderly watching, forgiving transgressions, shepherding the nation toward salvation. In Britain, the Church of England, in Egypt, Islam, in India, Hinduism. In New Zealand the media do the job, and even manage to declare a dividend on it.

You think of the media as a dynamic force, criticising, stimulating, questioning. Such organs do not transplant. The happy medians are a priesthood. When we doubt, they reassure the people; they comfort their isolation, assuage their uncertainties, remind them that all is for the best in the best of possible countries. The media's business is balm distribution, wholesale and retail. Overseas, the media criticise and question in a climate where all is not well. In New Zealand it is. The media can get on with their real job of reassurance.

Let's begin our survey of the varieties of religious experience with the established church, the New Zealand Broadcasting Corporation—to its intimates, 'the corp' (the se being silent). Where you come from a corporation is an independent organisation, like that centre of Black Power, the National Coal Board. Disabuse yourself. In New Zealand a corporation is a government department with freedom to choose its own letter-heads. In 1960 the National Party was anxious to present itself as the party of constitutional rectitude. It was also aware that television was coming, and could be more embarrassing for a government department to handle than, say, hydatids dosing. Yet the corporations can be troublesomely independent, whereas they should be seen and not heard. So the N.Z.B.C. was treated like the tamarillo (née tree tomato): the name was changed and the creature kept the same. Symbolically, Broadcasting House was built cowering beneath the Bowen State Building and hiding behind Parliament.

The N.Z.B.C. poses as much danger to the public peace as a Pekinese being taken out for walks on the end of a four inch steel cable. The corporation has to comply with any general or special directions given in writing by the minister, though since the minister responsible is usually the least literate, he prefers to pick up the telephone. Any telephone call reduces the N.Z.B.C. to jelly.

The Government rewards devoted servants of the National Party by appointing them to the corporation. Indeed if it appoints any more, they'll be able to form their own party branch. The only real qualification for the job is to have no knowledge of television. The corporation now appoints the Director-General, a daring innovation.

The whole structure is a new dimension of administrative theory. If ministers took out patent rights to it, they should be able to market the non-independent corporation to a British Conservative government, now moving much more clumsily in the same direction. The corporation does what is wanted without appearing to be told. If it does anything someone disapproves of, this can always be disavowed as a consequence of independence. If only show business had shown the same skill in developing the ventriloquist-less dummy.

Mark you, the whole structure is unnecessary. The corporation has no desire for independence. Overseas they speak of the immense power of television. In New Zealand we know its immense timidity, like a steamroller whose driver lives in terror of virus infection from the crowds milling under his wheels. Real freedom could be too much to bear; witness the state of desolation the corporation finds itself in when the government does naughty things like allowing privately controlled radio. Like a hysterical wife suspecting the husband she's been loyal to for forty years of adultery, the corporation alternates between hysterical plate throwing and even more hysterical self-abasement. Sometimes none of the poodle's tricks please. Imagine the consternation when you cancel the Brian Edwards Show and a minister promptly condemns you for it.

Yet don't fear a divorce. Conjugal bliss will return after the sulks. After all the corporation fears everyone else more than the government. Pressure groups protest at programmes or demand time; viewers write to the papers, or even ring the studios; M.Ps complain to the ministers; puritans protest about the sexual significance of showing the Apollo docking manoeuvre. The corporation has to protect itself against such a cruel world—by setting up Regional Advisory Committees.

Now representatives of every conceivable pressure group can air their views in confidence and this has a pacifying effect.

Another useful device is to leave the talking to the tame outsider who can always be disavowed in trouble. Hence the explanation of the meteoric rise of political science until it occupies much the same position as astrology in England.

The corporation needed outside experts. It couldn't use economists, who don't speak English; historians, whom even the N.Z.B.C. considers boring; or sociologists, because they simply put what everyone knows in language no one understands. The alternative was the political scientists. This worked well until suddenly it was discovered that, like lesser mortals, professors had opinions. The National Party detected that Robert Chapman was not 110 per cent sympathetic to them. I fell foul of the Labour Party by venturing to suggest that Norman Kirk was not God, though I guardedly added that he was still young. Each party promptly refused to accept its respective phobia to pontificate on its conference. The N.Z.B.C. honourably announced that it would not be dictated to. Of course it promptly dropped Chapman from the National Party conference and me from Labour's. This was because our socks smelled. Employment opportunities for political scientists were doubled overnight. Henceforth every commentator had to have a commentator to comment on him.

Finally, the ultimate deterrent: balance. Like Bishop Pompallier's house, this must be preserved at all costs. Did Mr Kirk get three-fifths of a second more than Mr Holyoake? Was one of Mr Watt's 625 lines missing? If the corporation misses a slip, stopwatches all over the country won't. So every script must be anxiously checked, every recording eagerly watched. In my day, programme production was divided into three parts: studio, control room and a greenroom filled with anxious officials. There they nervously watched a monitor, counting the letters in each word to make sure there were more than four, saying words backwards to see if they could be construed as dirty or an oblique criticism of Mr Muldoon.

Occasionally I would ask a question which departed from the prescribed routine of, 'Prime Minister, to what do you attribute the skill and dexterity and the amazing success with which you've handled the economic situation?' Off would go the studio lights. In would come a nervous director, 'Er, Austin, it's not me, but they'd like you to rephrase that question. Something a little more reverential might be appropriate. And you forgot to kneel.' One night, rumour had it that an alternative frontman had been standing by to be trundled in, in case I made any oblique criticism of the N.Z.B.C. The corporation issued a statement that the rumour was untrue. Later the alternative frontman thanked me for the overtime he had been paid for standing on call.

The final safeguard is the staffing system. Grown-up broadcasting organisations pay well. Talent is scarce and burns out quickly and they want the best. The N.Z.B.C. would run itself with volunteer labour, kept going by occasional mentions in *Relay*, had inconsiderate Nature not compelled employees to eat. As a generous compromise, minimum salaries are paid and strictly policed by the State Services Commission. So no one gets too powerful; the corporation is frightened of television personalities who might get too popular or too independent to play puppets. Like Brian Edwards, they have to go. This system excludes the talented, the energetic and other potential troublemakers. They can command more money elsewhere, digging drains or prestressing concrete dog kennels.

Those who remain are of two types. The lifers are the backbone of the organisation—modest men, which is entirely appropriate, long-time employees bringing the skills of radio announcing, accountancy and administration to the provision of chewing-gum for the eyes. All are pathetically loyal to a corporation they see as the last bulwark, defending the *Reader's Digest* and all that's best in life against crass commercialism. The other budding Cecil B. de Milles are trainees whose low wages are compensated for by the training they are receiving. They train, produce programmes, receive the ritual Feltex award (given for remaining in the country one calendar year), and then depart overseas to man the A.B.C., the

B.B.C. and I.T.V. The result is perhaps not the best, but certainly the most economical television system. New Zealand has the largest small studios in the world, a converted telephone booth there, a disused lift shaft here. Since no one with television experience is in a position of authority, expenditure can be kept low and expense in follies avoided: so N.Z.B.C. programmes are chiefly designed to give pleasure to accountants. Local television costs $6000 an hour, hard to beat even with home movies. If the second channel goes to the N.Z.B.C., it could be provided for by two new telecine machines, a videotape recorder and a part-time tea lady at Avalon.

The N.Z.B.C. is badly misunderstood, its officials assure me. It may not have provided professional local television, but it has been a competent importer and distributor of overseas programmes. It has brought the intellectual benefits of 'Coronation Street' to over 90 per cent of the population. It has provided a good service cheaply. It confers the additional blessing of Queen Mother substitutes in its continuity announcers. Above all it has developed the local martyr industry, processing for immortality such figures as St Scrimgeour and St Gordon the Resigned, and, with less acclaim, a whole host of minor saints, from St Keith of Aberdeen to Mike the Divine. Annually their feasts are commemorated by the Current Affairs Choristers, with the traditional madrigal, 'Oh Lord let our lips not speak that which in our hearts we know to be true', a refrain so gentle that no one can hear it.

Until 1970 the martyrs were all processed for the export market. Most of them went down well in Australia, which provided hope and comfort for those who believe in life after the N.Z.B.C. In the advent of commercial television, at least some martyrs would be able to stay at home for treatment, possibly even for reprocessing.

Naturally this is not the sole *raison d'être* of a second channel. It brings together a number of eminent men, whose ability at processing and canning and cinema running confers on them a unique capacity for controlling television, or at least running a pretty good all-knight party. With a whiff of channel number two, Dryden's dirigible waits to take the air, doubling the sum total of human happiness, the opportunity to see old American movies, and the employment opportunities for our tiny band of pundits.*

Once the basic problem of refining the high intellectual and cultural endeavour promised in its prospectus up to the purer forms of pap the people actually want, a private channel's prospects are good. If it communicates with the people as effectively as British commercial television, it should revolutionise the local scene. Yet with its older sister, private radio, it would bring a new and possibly undesirable intrusion into New Zealand life: competition. This is an alien beast the media have never met before.

The other section of the happy medians, the press, is well insulated from competition. About forty daily papers have a million circulation without needing to compete against each other. While the press is National, it is not national. Each paper has its own area, defined largely by geography with little overlap and less competition. In the main centres, readers have a choice between the political extremes of, say, the *Press,* an E.S.N. version of the London *Times,* and the *Christchurch Star,* Little Sir Echo to its Auckland sister. As in every other city they represent the political scene from right to extreme right. But this alternation is hardly competition. Nor do they compete for news, preferring to barter it through their own second-hand dealer, the Press Association, to guarantee that all the newspapers will print the same news at the same time. This encourages geographical mobility: people can move houses without seeing any differences in their paper. Truth is one and indivisible.

Absence of competition saves the readers from the worst aspects of the overseas press. That press feeds on tragedy; no business like woe business. It sensationalises. It unveils. John Delane once thundered that 'the press lives by disclosure'. Hunting out scandals, leading opinion, keeping up a feverish

---

* The Associated Network Group, the leading commercial contender for the second channel, announced in February 1972 that it would not apply for a warrant.

chatter of analysis and discussion. The press regards itself as a fourth estate.

The New Zealand press does none of these things. It is a business similar to the soft drinks industry. It buys news wholesale, dilutes it, makes it palatable with a little additional flavour, then retails it at inordinate profit. Like other New Zealand industries, it is uncompetitive and undynamic, protected against Lord Thomson or any other sort of change. Journalists' wages are kept low so that dangerous characteristics like too many ideas or too much initiative won't be encouraged. They aren't necessary where people have no choice of paper. Circulation is certain to grow as population grows. Not for New Zealand press lords the troubles of the British or American press. Profitability is guaranteed.

As a business, the press has its fortunes intimately bound up with its area, so becoming a local pressure group, pushing for development, defending local interests either with the hysterical inferiority complex of Dunedin papers, who see Otago's claims as rather like a harlot, never respected and frequently violated, or with the lofty superiority of Auckland. World War III would never make the main page in most small centres if it began on a day the Roads Board cut back the local programme.

The press is also a journal of record. Lists of wedding guests, the events at the Burnside Parent Teachers, the runners in the 3.30 must all be chronicled for posterity. So must the frequent statements of the pressure groups. Irrespective of style or sense, the statements must go in. 'New Zealand in danger', proclaims the R.S.A. speaking *ex cathedra,* as a Defence Department in exile. 'Power to the people', announces the M.E.D. Both will be reprinted with full acreage of text and an occasional correction to the spelling.

The press also acts as a forum. The correspondence columns show it at its fairest. Overseas papers filter out letters for such trivial reasons as incomprehensibility, incitement to riot, or obvious lunacy. In New Zealand all letters are equal. Being predominantly Protestant, the people don't believe in confession. Correspondence columns are the social safety valve. Such violent instincts as the desire to kill all people with long hair, to drown all graduates at birth, or canonise Mr Muldoon can all be sublimated anonymously instead of being bottled up or needing expensive psychological treatment. How sad that so few seize the opportunity to live out their violent instincts in print. To encourage the hesitant, here's a sample letter, certain of publication. Merely copy it out and attach your name.

Seacliff
21 October

Sir,
The defence of fluoridation from 'Mother of Sixteen' surely betrays his or her puerility and must cast doubts on her loyalty as well as his sanity. Close inquiry has shown that fluoridation is a communist plot. Small wonder it was advocated by that well known fellow traveller, Thomas Cook, and by Lord Keynes, the Italian Marxist. We are now paying the price of twenty years of communist influence in our educa-

tional system. Did not the Communist Party instruct its members to vote Labour in 1935 and did not the Labour Party appoint Dr Beeby, of whom Major Douglas has written, 'It's time we dropped the play-way and got back to basics'?

The answer lies in firm discipline and good wholesome food. In my day we were never allowed to gorge ourselves on lollies and pop. Corporal punishment firmly administered will drive back the tide of permissiveness which threatens to engulf us and which is directly to blame for the government's refusal to develop the airport at Wainakaroa for jumbo jets. We open ourselves too readily to the flood of foreign trash. It's time to reassert those basic New Zealand values for which our fathers died at Gallipoli. What would they have thought of long-haired louts betraying our boys in Vietnam?

ONE WHO FOUGHT FOR KING AND COUNTRY.

The overriding duty of the New Zealand press is that imposed on it by its unique responsibility to the Deity for the wellbeing of the nation. Now the second chamber is gone, it does this job alone. In foreign policy, editorials strike terror into the Chinese communists by vigorously defending American policy, whatever it happens to be. At home it asserts traditional values, warning that the world has been going downhill since the death of Massey and struggling to make New Zealand fit for Cobden and possibly even Bright to live in. Whatever is Right is right.

This imposes a higher duty than mere television. Where the N.Z.B.C. is so fickle as to be deferential to any government the people elect, the press is more responsible. As repository of the eternal interests of the nation, it sees that these can only be served by the National Party. Of course, as a free, vigorous and independent press, the papers from time to time have not to criticise the National Party, but to praise with faint damns—say, for the dullness of backbench teeth or the fact that only eighteen cabinet ministers have been to Backblocksville in the last two weeks. On these occasions the papers are never afraid to speak out responsibly. Yet the press believes in certain eternal values: 10 per cent unemployment, the dismantling of the welfare state. Where these verities and the policies of the National Party conflict, the dilemma is resolved in favour of the party, just as a Roman Catholic would opt for the Pope, and for similar reasons. Fortunately, too, all papers would resolve the dilemma in the same fashion. Editorials are all interchangeable since direct inspiration ensures that they all come from the same source. Witness the editorial on the eve of the election Kiwis are likely to be faced with if current economic trends continue:

'After the confusing claims and counter-claims of the last few weeks, the election tomorrow at last gives us the occasion for a clear decision and there can be little doubt that this should go in favour of the National Party.

'In its campaign of carping criticism, the Labour Opposition has dredged up every trivial accusation against the Government and all to no avail. Labour fails to see that a 25 per cent rate of unemployment has at last restored sanity to our economic system and incentives to those productive sections of the community anxious to make a contribution to the wellbeing of all.

'As for the accusation that inflation has now reached 32 per cent per annum, Labour seems to forget that inflation has been with us since the war under governments of both parties, while the present rate, though slightly higher than in the past, does give a considerable stimulus to invest. Anyone with a memory of 1957 will know the value of Labour's promises.

'We have never hesitated to criticise the National Party when it seemed right to do so. In the present situation we can only feel that the continuation in office of a National government under a man so experienced as the late Sir Keith Holyoake is absolutely imperative.

'The times are unusually difficult. National has a team of experienced ministers, and if they're a little elderly, this is surely a virtue when balance and wisdom are called for. Labour, on the other hand, threatens to risk all with untried experimentation and premature, unnecessary and expensive demands for change. As in the past its policies have been weighed and found wanting. Its leaders, having not held office for many years, can know little of the working of a modern economy and are certainly not qualified to deal with a moment of danger like the present.

'We are confident that the electorate will plump not for irresponsibility but for statesmanship and, just in case they don't, we will continue to ensure that the National Party, in power or in opposition, continues to control the destinies of our nation.'

In editorials no one reads, the press preaches its eternal values.

The press has done its job of guaranteeing social stability magnificently. A sensationalist press would have created discontent by unearthing scandals or making people think all was not well. The New Zealand press prefers the safe. Familiarity breeds content. Scandals such as police corruption in the 1950s, the state of the mental hospitals in the 1960s, corruption in import licences have to be forced on the press. It prefers to let lying dogs sleep.

Overseas tabloids are like *Playboy* in monochrome and could well come with serviettes to wipe away the drool. By contrast, *Truth,* the peeping tom's *Listener,* is clear and fresh as a menthol smoker's lung. It manages a circulation of a quarter of a million under plain cover. Vice-chancellors do not read it of course—though they sometimes change their staff appointments on its recommendation. *Truth* in its capacity as the literary branch of the Security Service has turned the smear into an artform. Its portraits of Dr Finlay, Phil Holloway and Brian Edwards all fetched high prices. Coms, particularly Com Poms, tremble at its voice. The paper can be relied on to expose fearlessly anyone too harmless to hit back. Institutions it will only take on if they are unpopular, otherwise it attacks them through people, as in the Edwards case: the people's Brian was in the firing line simply because *Truth* was having a be-nasty-to-the-N.Z.B.C. week. In compensation, *Truth* will do Frank Brutal exposures (when Frank's in town) of anything which titivates on the lines of,

'Is abortion a labour-saving device?' 'Can nudism cure cancer?' (with pictures).

Other examples of muckraking journalism are to be found in *Straight Furrow,* and community harmony is sometimes disrupted by the organ of the National Association of Bird Fanciers, *Cock.* Fortunately, once the price of the *New Zealand Woman's Weekly* went up few could spare the extra for *Cock.* As for the Left, its periodicals sometimes come and mainly go. *Here and Now* is dead and gone, *Tomorrow* is yesterday, the *New Zealander* went after nine issues and *Dispute* hardly lasted much longer. Only the *Monthly Review* carries on, thanks to a strict policy of publishing the same articles but changing the dates. It gets a somewhat masochistic pleasure from warning of a capitalist coup which is always incipient yet never materialises.

Whatever the critics might say, New Zealand has flourishing and diverse media. Just look how many different treatments you would get for the same event, say a national emergency. Imagine that on one of the rare visits of Prince Philip, the royal trousers fell down in the middle of Cathedral Square, Christchurch.

N.Z.B.C. TV NEWS. Christchurch cameraman having been reloading at the time, features library film of last royal visit to Cathedral. Commentary by Ian Johnstone. Followed by interview with eyewitness, Mrs Ethel Gittings, aged eighty-four. Film scratched in hurried processing. Mrs Gittings possibly out of sync, though this could be due to age.

SECOND CHANNEL. Shots of the backs of heads and interview with eyewitness, Mrs Ethel Gittings, seventy-two. Followed by re-enactment in which roving reporter's trousers fall down in Queen St. Commentary by Barry Crump. This is then followed by rescreening of 1933 movie *Frankenstein and Dracula Meet the National Council of Women.*

N.Z.B.C. BRIAN EDWARDS SHOW. Brian Edwards lowered on to set on throne of burning gold. Cracks four jokes from *N.Z.B.C. Joke Book* (rebound copy of *Punch* for 1912). Mr Muldoon's trousers pulled down by T. Shadbolt, C. Wheeler and A. Taylor. Mr Muldoon emerges triumphant. Programme not screened because of possible libel of Sir George Grey (*ob.* 1893) and Emperor Franz Josef of Austria (*ob.* 1912).

N.Z.B.C. CHECKPOINT. Interview with editor of *Court Circular* over wire from London on precedents for royal trousers falling down. Chairman of New Zealand Association of Gyroscope Manufacturers brought in for balance. Final comment from Dr Sutch who attributes incident to dismantling of import licensing.

N.Z.B.C. COUNTRY CALENDAR. Secretary of Federated Farmers, Pryde, and vice-chairman of the New Zealand Wool Board, Prejudice, discuss 'Can wool face the emerging challenge?'

N.Z.B.C. GALLERY. Panel discussion, including Rev. Bob Lowe, Winston McCarthy, Denis Glover and secretary, New Zealand Federation of Braces Manufacturers (who announces in a plea so moving that New Zealand Express would have been proud of it that the braces concerned were imported).

STATION 3Y.C. Interview with Arthur Higgins who once served in the same frigate as Prince Philip but never actually spoke to him.

RADIO HAURAKI. News flash, followed by Andy Stewart singing 'Donal, Where's Your Trousers'.

CHRISTCHURCH PRESS. 'Royal Tour Voted Success'. Accompanied on his way by the Bishop of Christchurch and the Mayor, the Duke paused as he came out of the Cathedral, to make a characteristically friendly gesture to the crowd outside. The keynote of informality and humanity which has characterised the present tour was seen by all in Christchurch, and the city responded with its usual enthusiasm. The whole scene was splendidly set off by the Cathedral itself, described by a previous royal visitor, Edward VIII, as among the most magnificent pieces of Anglican Ecclesiastical architecture in the Southern Hemisphere.

OTAGO DAILY TIMES EDITORIAL. The incident in Christchurch, though inflated out of all proportion, demonstrated once again the justice of our earlier criticism of the itinerary which ministers saw fit to devise for the royal party. Had Dunedin been treated in the same way as cities of equal importance such as Auckland, the royal couple would not have been in Christchurch at the time of the incident but in Dunedin.

CHRISTCHURCH STAR. What could have been an embarrassing incident was quickly turned into humour by the Duke who quipped, 'I'd better belt up.' The Bishop led the large crowd in hearty laughter and the tour proceeded.

AUCKLAND STAR. What could have been an embarrassing incident was quickly turned into humour by the Duke, who quipped, 'I'd better belt up.' The Bishop led the large crowd in hearty laughter and the tour proceeded.

EVENING STAR, DUNEDIN. The Christchurch sun shone brightly for the Duke. The city was ablaze with blossom trees. In the words of the poet, 'Earth has not very much to show more fair'.

DOMINION. Duke of Edinburgh Observed in Christchurch: Flash.

TRUTH. 'Duke and Ethel Gittings: Rumours denied'. A police officer yesterday recalled Ethel Gittings' red associations. She never spoke out against the 1951 wharf strike of which the Prime Minister, Sid Holland, said, 'This is communist conspiracy at its most flagrant.' In 1954 she walked within a hundred yards of a Progressive Bookshop and is believed to have travelled on the same train as Vic Wilcox, General Secretary of the Communist Party. With tears in her eyes, an ordinary New Zealand mother told me today, 'We should kick women like that out of the Plunket Society.' To the Duke, *Truth* says, 'Drop it, Phil'.

NEW ZEALAND WOMAN'S WEEKLY. Once again the Duke created the happiest impression by his breezy informality. Afterwards Mrs Ethel Gittings (ninety-eight) said, 'It was the happiest moment of my life.'

SUNDAY NEWS. 'Ethel Gittings: "Now I've seen it all".'

MONTHLY REVIEW. 'That children from the state schools were unable to witness the incident because the authorities had seen fit to put seried ranks of Christ's College boys in front, demonstrates once again the socially discriminatory planning which has characterised this entire tour.' Followed by an article showing that the underpants production is up 248 per cent in Cuba since the revolution. This in turn is followed by further fairy tales from North Vietnam, 'where bombs drop, not trousers'.

COCK (SPECIAL). 'The whole world watches: Cock Special'. Two hundred and forty-eight authenticated examples of police deliberately putting their groins in the way of the innocent boots of demonstrators. Also a hundred and sixty-eight cases of police eating garlic and breathing on crowds.

LISTENER. 'If the notion is once accepted that the camera is doing its job by permitting viewers to see that which is better not to be seen, we are well on the way towards a species of television that misses entirely the civilising potential of our electronic age. We have been too short a time in the game to surrender the new medium to such exhibitionism, however excusable, instead of developing television in absorbing and socially useful ways.'

Whatever the differences of approach, all share the common attribute of mediocrity. None can compare with the best of overseas television or newspapers. Their defence is that they don't sink as low as the worst, an answer which in itself indicates a condescending stodginess. Overseas newspapers and television appeal to a defined market, and set out to cater for it professionally. This gives them a clear-cut stance and character to suit the market, where Kiwi papers have to be all things to all men and more of them to the National Party. Overseas tabloid newspapers are miracles of communication —simplifying, ordering, selecting, to put over information in the language of their audience. Quality papers do the same for a higher social group. The New Zealand media must cater for a universal audience. So they fall between every possible stool, too staid and elaborate for the masses, too simplified and superficial for the élite. And not professional enough for either. Communication—through pap television, inquiring quality journalism, or screaming tabloid headlines —is a matter of professionalism, knowing the audience and speaking directly to it in the way best calculated to be heard. This professionalism has never fully developed, partly because the able leave, mainly because neither press nor television has been prepared to attract and retain excellence. Lack of competition has given little incentive to do so. It is easier to play safe, be cautious and avoid problems. News is unattractively presented under unappetising headlines, film interviews are badly edited, speeches are served up cold by reprinting the official handout, and the tiny parliamentary lobby keeps in with ministers by reprinting what they want. Any departure from this norm and their sources would dry up anyway. And until the nation is bigger, more variegated, more professional, so it has to be.

A few foreign diet substitutes are permissible. The *News of the World* is available for those who crave the timeless verities of 'Teenage Brain Surgeon in Naked Mercy Dash to Palace Corgi, Court Told'. *Time* is an adequate preparation for those C.I.A. extension courses, the university American studies prescriptions. The *Reader's Digest* may be the most forgettable magazine you've ever read, but it will enable you to make a considerable conversational impact at the Jaycees and even in the university commonroom.

Anything else would be dangerous. I know a professor who had the *Guardian* flown in on ice, another who kept his air-mail *Observer* unopened until he could read it in bed on Sunday.

Avoid this. The consequences are damaging to your sense of reality. Imagine for example the Conservative Party's 1970 election victory in Britain as it would be reported in New Zealand:

DAY ONE. Hear the news on N.Z.B.C. steam radio and first analysis by senior lecturer in political science at Victoria University. He is clearly surprised by the whole thing, but manages to talk about unexpected nineteenth century election results.

DAY TWO. Read news in morning papers, illustrated by photograph of Wilson taken 1949 and Heath departing for Brussels 1962. Result discussed in editorial. Editor clearly torn between his relief that Right has triumphed and his unspoken knowledge that a Conservative government could be disastrous for New Zealand, since Conservatives want to go into Europe, sell New Zealand to Lee Kuan Yew as a joint base, and detain all New Zealanders travelling to Britain in the same prisons as Kenyan Asians. Conflict resolved by commending the British people for their decisive rejection of the outdated notions of socialism.

DAY FOUR. See film on N.Z.B.C. television. James Callaghan wrongly described as Enoch Powell.

DAY FIVE. Read first overseas analysis of election result in airmail edition of *Economist*. Begin to understand but too late to be any use.

DAY THIRTY-FIVE. Read final days of campaign and results and comment in badly torn surface mail copies of *Guardian*. Wonder when it all happened.

Many expatriate Englishmen suffer from such intellectual time lapse. Events begin to blur into each other. Life becomes a series of flashbacks, like seeing the same film six times, each time longer, each time less interesting.

Avoid the danger. Read only the New Zealand papers. Your acclimatisation will accelerate. It's dangerous to have overseas ideas and opinions smuggled in, however plain the cover. Unless you absorb events through New Zealand newspapers which reduce everything to the same level of unreality, you'll never acquire that sense of remoteness and insulation which is the hallmark of the true New Zealander.

Seriously I don't want to seem critical. After all the media in New Zealand are the best in the world. They'll tell you so at regular intervals. And just in case you don't believe them, they'll take advertising space to second the motion.

THE KULTURE
of the KIWI BIRD

CRITICS TALK of a land without culture. Ignore the internal ones: inspiring a little collective guilt is as good a way of making a living as any other and *Landfall* and the N.Z.B.C. are both willing to subsidise the sermons which are the bulk of their cultural output. External critics are more savage. When I left for New Zealand friends loaded me with scratched classical records and magazine reproductions of Constable as if for a life sentence on Desert Island Discs or a tour as cultural missionary to Morrinsville. Those with military backgrounds jeered, 'It's one big sergeants' mess' or 'I could always pick the Kiwis in the '44 Italian campaign—we looted the paintings and they went for the booze and car spares'. An expatriate discerned two types of New Zealander, those associating culture with home brewing and those spelling it with a K.

All this makes the Kiwis reach for their cultural census statistics. They produce more culture per acre and consume more per capita than any country, except possibly Ancient Greece (and the Greeks were morally suspect). New Zealanders read more books than any other nation, even if *Best*

Bets inflates the total. And culture isn't confined to one class, for there is cultural book-spreading. Proletarian poems pour into *Woman's Weekly*. Old ladies enter the Kelliher painting competition. They usually win, too.

All this will be trotted out quicker than praise of the government from Tourist and Publicity, or criticism from the Government Statistician. So don't put anyone to the trouble. Just attempt a deeper understanding. New Zealand is a cultural layer cake. C. P. Snow discerned two cultures. It has three.

First, take the Everidges. Theirs is a genuinely New Zealand way of life. Satirists can quickly characterise it just by reeling off such trigger words as half-G, T.A.B. or state house. These people don't have to worry about the state of New Zealand culture, so they are the only genuinely happy section. Secure in the knowledge that they are better off than most, their happiness isn't disturbed by thoughts of Vietnam or poverty in the Indus Basin. To get on with them, increase

your beer capacity, memorise the maintenance manual for some outdated Ford, and don't mention culture: it will only produce embarrassment, mimicry of posh accents and deliberate mispronunciations. Their approach to culture is similar to that of an Egyptian army to the Israelis, only faster. As far as they're concerned, Plato is a metal polish. A trendy Auckland boutique calling itself Art Nouveau had thousands of them dropping in to ask after Art's health. At the University of Otago, building workers on the library who were asked to keep the noise down as people were working replied that they had seen no sign of working, just a few blokes reading books. University staff were convulsed each of the 2,987,641 times this story was told. The same atitude emerges in the advert in the Greymouth paper, 'Exchange piano for something useful'. In language your Everidge is a man of few words, a lot of them 'bloody'.

Think of an Englishman, and a figure with a Savile Row suit, bowler and umbrella furled as tightly as his copy of *The Times* springs to mind. Think of a Kiwi, and he wears a check shirt, an eight-ounce glass, a vacant grin and a trilby at the back of the head. The British stereotype is middle class, the Kiwi is proletarian, a sure indication of which group sets the tone. Where the middle classes dominate Britain, the Kiwi counterparts feel themselves an alienated minority, keeping alight the lamp of civilisation and staying in touch with the main army through the regular bulletins of *Vogue, Reader's Digest* or the rash of part publications on music, history or antiques, these last being distinct from most foreign magazines which now concentrate on private part publication.

They are the Respectables. As islands of respectability in a philistine sea they have to differentiate themselves from the slobocracy which surrounds them. This means suits for the men and a uniform of hat and gloves for the women. It means drinking wine instead of beer. (In theory the nation consumes one gallon per head per year; in practice it mostly vanishes down middle class gullets.) It means voting National. It means remodelling the house on ideas from *Homes and Gardens* and furnishing it with pirated copies of Swedish

furniture. They view popular culture with a vague distaste. Because the puritan ethic still lingers they equate dullness with respectability, an explanation of the state of the press. The ethic also produces savings and personal insurance through endowment policies and regular churchgoing, an outward and visible symbol of an inner respectability. They patronise local culture to the extent of buying occasional items from the booming nicknackery shops, or even reproductions of prints by the third-rate artists employed by the New Zealand Company to give a raw country a veneer of respectability. Yet they really prefer imported culture, because, if other people approve, it must be O.K. As a university lecturer you'll be greeted warmly as an ally from cultural HQ. They'll nervously inquire whether you're called doctor and be honestly puzzled by the drunken passes you make at their daughter. Keep your revolting habits to yourself, tell them they have a charming home and all will be well, even possibly the daughter.

The third group are the Intellectuals. The Respectables

react against the masses below them; Intellectuals react against the Respectables. They wouldn't dream of living near the Everidges and they're not sure how to talk to them, but they do imitate enough of the Everidge life style to shock the Respectables with a carefully controlled casualness about dress, behaviour and language. Two slurred 'bloody's' per hundred words and you're talking to an Everidge; none and you've hit a Respectable; five clear and distinct ones and he's an Intellectual. Adjust your own bloody output to keep pace. Another guide is television: Intellectuals often don't have one, either because they're too busy appearing on it to watch, or because they haven't been asked. Don't expect intellectual conversation. Intellectuals are too busy mowing down wild pigs, building houses or sailing boats to prove their normality —they have no time to read books like their overseas counterparts.

Jack, Jonathan and John look in different cultural directions. Jack averts his gaze, being preoccupied with the three o'clock race; Jonathan looks to overseas whence cometh his *Time* magazine; John spends his time pulling New Zealand culture up by the roots to inspect growth. Nowhere has the dawn of a national culture been so much discussed, so often heralded, so frequently postponed. Some day my culture will come.

Yet the soil isn't naturally fertile. Pastoral poets and painters haven't developed where man is a camper on an alien landscape, baffled by its beauty rather than sharing its moods. Seasons, which dictate a cycle of life and literature overseas, are a steady sameness. Where tension and conflict produce cultural vigour, there is uniformity. The Taihape tearooms are no substitute for the salons of eighteenth century France and instead of concentrating culture, New Zealanders have to spread it. If Dargaville can't have its grand opera and Waimate its Ballet Royale no one shall have them. The New Zealand Players exhausted themselves spreading Ariel by topdressing to a score of centres, a mistake neatly repeated by the Great New Zealand Theatre Revival (Mark II) in 1966. The country's symphony orchestra is a collection of cultural commercial travellers who do 100 miles to the concerto, the highest m.p.c. in musical history.

Smallness makes this a good place for the ordinary bloke, a bad one for the culture vulture. It makes the place a cultural province and means that New Zealand themes and subjects are of little interest to a wider world. Artists, writers and painters go unrecognised. Most of New Zealand's best writing has been done overseas, which either focuses the mind on essentials or suffuses reality with the roseate glow Katherine Mansfield saw. Most of the worst writing has been done *for* abroad. This means explaining everything as if for a class of half-wits, and cramming in four Maoris, two tuis and a bellbird every ten pages. Alternatively it means adding to the mound of general books about New Zealand, all of them boiled down and updated versions of the *Yearbook*.

The market is too small to allow many to make a living from culture. There is no wealthy élite to patronise it and it isn't tax deductible. So culture needs crutches and the government has to provide them. This produces two dangers: sponsoring prestige projects, and institutionalising caution:

> I've been all over this country
> And one thing is clear to me
> It's the mushroom that grows in the open field
> The toadstool under the tree.

Neither danger has been avoided. There will never be a Kiwi *Ulysses* and *Portnoy* would not get beyond the manuscript.

There is no high culture. Yet if the mountains are too remote there has been activity in the foothills. The writers have made a good start at literature with poetry and short stories, even if the Great New Zealand Novel remains unwritten. The nation has produced good character actors, but no great all-rounder; exquisite short films, even if the feature film hasn't been a runaway success. Some nice houses, no great building.

What Kiwis do have is a flourishing low culture. Art, drama and music are branches of do-it-yourself. With fewer writers, artists and musicians, they have more writing, art and music because everyone produces, even those with neither qualifications nor ability. Excellence isn't likely—you can't have a do-it-yourself Academie Francais or a backgarden Bolshoi. Yet what's the point of excellence. It might embarrass. The Timaru Thespians aren't trying to dig undiscovered truth from Beckett's dustbins but to keep themselves amused. The audience is there out of a sense of duty, with the additional draw of seeing Auntie Ethel or old George make fools of themselves. As for the reviewer, unless his reactions are hysterically favourable, then his job is in danger, possibly his life. Criticism can be reserved for artists from overseas who are paid to take it.

New Zealand also has a flourishing popular literature, the only field outside plastic tiki production in which Develop-

ment Conference targets have been exceeded. A growing share of books sold are printed in the country and writers of all kinds stand a better chance of being published than anywhere else outside Gestetnerland. They mustn't attempt literature: this reflects reality, transmuting it into art. It could reveal the stresses and tensions behind outward small town stability. It might hold up a mirror. A dangerous pursuit.

In 1967 I visited Blackball, envisaging a film on *Coal Flat Revisited*. It quickly emerged that Pearson's return would provide only the raw material for New Zealand's first lynching. The declining mining community found the portrayal of its life of twenty years ago unforgivable. Pearson would have done better to write a civic brochure with photographs of the houses, perhaps the school. Mention the name of Janet Frame in Oamaru and conversation turns to eccentricities, and breakdowns, real or imagined. Writing won't come up.

These are the dangers of real literature. Popular literature is much nicer. It shows the Kiwi as he wants to be seen rather than as he is. It helps him to escape from reality. Who buys natural yoghurt now it comes in a whole range of flavours?

So the Kiwi humour book portrays a sweet and lovable character. The sports book, the literary equivalent of Batman, portrays him as mighty. The backblocks book, history, and romance all allow readers to escape. All they lack is the Kiwi thriller, or Kiwi science fiction, to chronicle the strange events at the Kaiwai pig breeding station, or Kiwi pornography, perhaps taking up the same subject.

Sports literature is a 'strip' comic. If the sportsmen spoke their minds they'd be silent, so they usually have the help of a ghost, a spiritual kind of journalist, who also writes all the other sports books. Whatever their genre, sports writers are men of such potency they can make the platitude pregnant and turn the cliché into an art form. The sportsman's

basic grunt is translated into purple prose, best described as spheroid baroque. Observe this cunning build-up of suspense:

'If you were alive and taking an interest in sport in 1928 you will know that the big mystery was, "Why isn't Mark Nicholls in the test team against South Africa?" Four tests were played . . . but Mark Nicholls who had been named as the brains of the All Blacks in 1924 . . . played in just one test. In that test, the final one, he scored 10 of New Zealand's 13 points. Yes, why wasn't Mark Nicholls played in more tests?'

The suspense is unbearable. Did Nicholls have Maori blood? Did intelligence make him suspect? To continue:

'I asked Mark that not so long ago and he just grinned and remarked that apparently he wasn't considered good enough.' Edgar Wallace has a lot to learn.

In the same way the tour accounts, literary videotape libraries, improve on Nordic myth. Verbal action replays are padded out by anecdotes about the players, the officials and the country which had the misfortune to fall victim to them. The real story of the drinking, debauching and wenching isn't told because that would be the province of literature proper. If sporting books were either accurate or critical, the subjects might not buy them and in a small market the loss of sales to a whole team could be crucial. So sportsmen always emerge as honest, God-fearing thugs with no trace of libido, conceit or intellect, just Kiwis who happen to run faster, jump higher or knee-groin more deftly than average.

Occasionally prose is transmuted into poetry:

'Caduceus, the fabulous midget from Downunder, must be the greatest living horse the world over. In fact if Jack Litten had been there to throw the reins of Caduceus to Richard III when that desperate tyrant shrieked his entreaty for "A horse, a horse, my kingdom for a horse", the whole fabric of history might have been woven of an entirely different yarn.'

Kiwi humour comes in many forms: Crump, Crumpette, *The Kiwi Laughs, Hansard, The Half-gallon Jar, From N to Z*. All skilfully blend the tragic vision of P. G. Wodehouse with the comic sense of Emily Brontë. They achieve their point by manipulation of stereotypes—the honest Kiwi har-

assed by an oppressive government machine, weighed down by taxes, surviving on his wits. In Dunedin he wears a kilt, in the country gumboots or a gun, elsewhere a brown skin. Most are politically paternalist, except for Crump, the very best of them and the only man to emerge from the back-blocks who can actually write. He retells, in vivid vernacular, tales that are legend in the bush. With such natural food for fun as dogs strangling themselves, shooting accidents, grub-eating Maoris and drunken escapades, Crump strikes just the right note for his countryman's sophisticated sense of humour. His book output keeps neck and neck with Apollo launchings.

Crumperature overlaps into the escapism of the backblocks book, whether it be about pioneer history, high country life or hill life in the raw as in *A Husband in the House*. All help citizens to escape the dull routine of suburban existence, and sublimate the guilt they feel about their accumulated consumer durables by recreating the simple life on high country farm or backblocks hut, where existence is straightforward, simple and incredibly boring, rather like the people who live it. At its worst the genre can be reduced to a list of furniture, or in the history books a compilation of names. Everyone gets a thrill at the mention of some imagined ancestor:

'When Brown and Maud sold Ashwick to Cyril Hawdon and Alexandér Strachey in 1871 the station extended from the Opihi to the Opuha rivers . . . Strachey, who became manager of the station, named it Ashwick after his Somerset home, Ashwick Grove, Oak Hill. He was a relative of the English author John St Lee Strachey . . . Cyril Hawdon was the son of Joseph Hawdon of Craigie Burn Station, North Canterbury, who drove the first mob of cattle from New South Wales to Adelaide. Hawdon and Strachey held Ashwick for only a year when they sold it and later bought Westerfield Station from the executors of Charles Reed for £62,000. Twenty thousand sheep went with him.'

If only sheep could read, the entire 20,000 would have been mentioned by name, too. Until they can the honour is reserved for the dogs.

Bush literature is for men, history for families, romantic novels for women. They are written in New Zealand but often printed overseas so that they have to be decked out with pakeha girls who turn out to be Maori princesses, slightly faded, or Maoris who turn out to be pakeha princes when the last chapter reveals them as doctors' sons. Difficulties have to be heightened to build up tension before the predictable ending:

'"Things are not going too well at Wharewai," replied Mrs

Hewitt a little sadly. "Randie spends too much time in Napier and like men everywhere and natives in particular work slackens off a lot. There have been other things, too; a late frost in November killed off the early plums, the tomatoes and the early potatoes. Leaf curl is rampant this season and the strange weather we are having just now is killing off the cows in hundreds with bloat and the sheep with pulpy kidneys. To wind things up properly Randie bought a new and very expensive grader—valuable but not of immediate necessity." '

Worry not, love will out.

Popular literature provides an indirect and accidental, but nonetheless compelling, picture of the Kiwi. The English seek sublimation in James Bond, connoisseur of wine, usually white, and women, usually red. New Zealanders escape into the bush, where man pits himself against nature not other men, even stock and station agents. A nation tied down to jobs, families and mortgages sublimates on the myth of the free man, Sam Cash. Not a dirty thought disturbs this literature for it is marketed, not only to be read, but also to be given or bought by the yard to furnish blonded pine bookshelves. If it isn't clean it can't be displayed and people will give each other toilet soap for Christmas.

Sex does not exist. America has produced the adultery novel in *The Philanderer,* the masturbation novel in *Portnoy,* and the wife-swapping novel in *Couples.* They would have produced the necrophilia novel if it weren't a dying art. The exertion of re-living hundreds of rugby matches, re-enacting the death of thousands of deer leaves our populace too tired for sex. Literature stops at the bedroom door.

It's also a literature of male domination. Women are objects to be escaped from, or homely homemakers cooking and providing for the hero and bearing his children. Nowhere is there any feeling for, or understanding of, the female of the species, even when a woman is the author. Woman is a stylised creature dragged in for a few mumbled words of thanks for being so long-suffering with husbands who are really married to rugby, running, or the farm. Occasionally a woman qualifies for the same companionship as the dog or

the horse. Marriage and honeymoons are awkward jokes. The few examples of genuine emotion occur between men and men, or men and animals.

Unfortunately, too, the literature is limited in range and subject. More variety is needed. If possible it should be provided in the one multi-purpose book to avoid the expense of having to buy so much to get a complete coverage. Fairburn once argued that the Great New Zealand Novel would be about a kindly man with a wife and ten boys aged between nine and twelve years who happens to discover (entirely by accident presumably) that his wife is really a man. To my humble mind it would be more complex, a story that could be filmed as our second full-length feature flop, *Carry on Running Away,* with Peter Sellers playing three million roles as the entire population of New Zealand. The story would go something like this.

Chapter I

Melinda's dark eyes flashed as she glanced round the tiny kitchen which had been her home ever since Jim had brought her there, that happy autumn day when the leaves had been golden and the river had reflected the blue of the sky, rather than the sullen grey colour she saw now. Oh that river, how she hated it. Cutting her off from the neighbours, from the world outside, and worst of all from her mother in Christchurch. Yet sometimes she loved it, marking the boundary of the little world she and Jim had made their own. Perhaps one day they'd have a son to share their world. She mused as the stew for the hands simmered merrily on the stove. The parrot nodded drowsily on his perch and Beth and old Mick barked outside, obviously anticipating an early lunch.

Idly she began to think of the morning's events. Funny old Hori taking her off to Redstar station to see that aerial thing. Even odder the way Bert O'Tsung had reacted, shouting at her to get off his land and leave him alone. He'd never quite fitted in since he'd arrived the year before —why Jim said he didn't even attend the Federated Farmers meetings!

No one had a clue how he managed Redstar station without running a single sheep. Still it was none of her business, she thought. Live and let live was the only thing with neighbours, as Jim said.

In any case what would Jim say when she told him about Mum's letter and the news that Nadine had run away from St Margaret's with a Maori boy. Ah, there was Jim—she could hear the Landrover coming down the valley. Time to put the scones in the oven. She took the griddle from the gleaming sink top and slipped it into the oven . . .

Jim heard the explosion half a mile away. It could only have been the house—and that hole in the roof. Melinda— was she all right? His heart beat faster, a cold sweat formed on his hands. Hurtling down the road he dashed into the smoking wreck of the kitchen. 'Darling, darling, what . . .' 'Hori,' was all she said as the book on flower arrangement slipped from her hand. He closed her stew-sodden eyelids. Melinda was dead.

Chap II
Py Kori, they're funny blokes my pakeha neighbours. Spend all their time at their boring meetings when they could be sitting on the veranda watching the sunset with a nice half-G. Even better, looking through old T.A.B. slips. Cardigan Bay—now there was a horse!

Never get all the kids in the V8 soon. Never mind she'll be right. Lets get 3ZB on the trannie. Wonder if Bert could

get it on that plurry aerial affair. Don't really know why
it's necessary—the trannie can get 2ZB as well and that's
enough for any man. No need for him to be so angry when
he'd seen us watching—and that coot with him, the one
with the earphones. Could swear that was Jack Jankers,
first-five for Northland. Boy did I get drunk the night they
won the shield. But this beer—this beer's off. Better take it
back . . .

Jim found him lying where he'd fallen. 'Hori, what happened?' The half-G crashed to the ground. 'Jack Jankers.
Py Kori', was all he said.

Chap III

It's very rarely that a practice game really 'comes alive'
but in Dargaville they still talk about that game at the
beginning of March when W. L. 'Hoppy' Johnson's team
more than met their match in a team fielded by Arthur
'Scratch' Jones. In the annals of rugby many games are
embossed in gold. This one deserved carving on the portals
of the rugby Pantheon. They rucked and scrummed under
the warm autumn sun, and only a Tolstoy of rugby could
do justice to the game. Just ask any of the friendly Northland folk and they'll tell you. Perhaps they'll begin with
that scrum in the third minute when 'Hoppy' Johnson
streaked away with the ball to dodge 'Miffy' Thompson
and two others before passing to Big Jim Malloy to score.
They're arguing still about whether Big Jim was offside but
I'll go along with the man in the crowd who shouted, 'Well
done Jim.' Perhaps they'll tell you about T. S. 'Mucker'
Mitchell's magnificent conversion with a light wind blowing from the east and the fleecy clouds flitting across the
face of the soft autumn sun as the ball soared high over the
posts. The crowd went wild with delight. Or they may tell
you about that free-wheeling ruck just before half-time when
A. J. 'Red Fed' Jankers bent for the ball and a boot connected with his head. Whose boot it was we'll never know.
No one in those two magnificent teams of fine New Zealanders would have been capable of such an act. Perhaps
'Red Fed' told the man who ran out from the crowd to him,
but those nearby only heard this mysterious stranger mutter, 'Where's Bert?' Jack gasped, 'Ranfurly Shield. Watch
the Ref.' But that's just what they say. The final whistle
had blown for a great five-eighth. Jack Jankers had gone
to join the big game in the sky. At Dargaville the spirit
had gone out of the play but the match continued to a
30-30 draw.

Chapters IV-X—Condensed version

The chase continues from Dargaville. Following up the mysterious last words of Jankers, Jim Spence is compelled to attend every Ranfurly Shield match. This provides a chance to reprint the entire teams, the names of the referees and linesmen, attendance figures and prevailing weather conditions. Finally a referee is killed by a poisoned boot stud and dies, warning Spence to 'Beware the Lions', then by coincidence touring New Zealand. At two test matches Spence discovers that messages are being passed from mouth to mouth during scrums. He captures one. Uncoded by one of the few loyal university lecturers, it leads to the unveiling of a plot to infiltrate the entire Rugby Union. The traitors are weeded out by W. E. 'Brig' Gilbert and his trained hookers, listening in every scrum for disloyal conversation.

The subversion threat then shifts to an attempt to destroy New Zealand's recently purchased fleet of forty ex-government surplus Graf Zeppelins by puncturing them with flying cricket stumps. This allows a ball by ball analysis of three matches, complete with team photographs and extracts from the programme. Eventually the two ringleaders are eliminated, one hit on the head by a fast baller from the security service, the other succumbing to an unusually dry wicket in Auckland.

Spence is now well on the trail of his former neighbour. He follows him through New Plymouth, a pretty city of sturdy independent-minded people (colour photo), Hastings, a pretty town with a population sturdy in its independence (colour photo), and Christchurch, the most English of New Zealand cities (photo of Government Life Building). In Dunedin Bert O'Tsung is found to have been spearheading a Chinese attempt to tap the Speights branch of New Zealand Breweries. The danger that the population of China might grow up big and virile on these illicit supplies is soon averted, and clues then lead to Piecookaorangi, Block 19. After two attempts to poison Spence with antlers dipped in industrial effluent, the fugitive stumbles on a high country station. There, in a smoke-filled room replete with such characters as 'Old Bill', whose fathers and forefathers have been in the back country ever since they dodged the draft in 1949, he learns how to skin and cook in mud one of his dogs, which has been accidentally shot.

(The recipe follows.)

Chapter XI

The weather couldn't make up its mind to soak us or just freeze us to death. Back in the hut the cooking pots rattled and the new bloke prattled. Odd that he's not stopped talking for eight weeks now, but Ken said he was a good keen man. And Ken should know, even if he's only managed to shoot a bit of pork and two dogs since he came.

Bert mused idly, rifle in his lap. Then he spotted Jim striding up the ridge, rifle at the ready, bush hat pushed back. Bert rose. The two men paced out the distance between them. Not a word was spoken. Bolts clicked. Thirty yards. Beads were drawn. Twenty yards. They couldn't miss. Suddenly, with one thought, both threw down their rifles. Stumbling towards each other they embraced. They were dancing, swinging each other round with glad cries of 'Jim', 'Bert', 'How's the station', 'How's the heap', 'How's the wife', 'Well, I never could stand her cooking', 'Mate', 'Mate'.

Arm in arm they walked into the sunset. The mist was rising in the bush as the Southern Cross gazed impassively down. From the gully came the cry of a lone kakapo. Night was falling.

OVERSEASIA

A SPECTRE IS HAUNTING New Zealand. It is the spectre of Overseasia. Like sex you can forget it for a time; in the long run you can't do without it. Three million people can't cultivate their garden without the occasional peek over the fence at the three thousand million jostling outside. Being small makes Kiwis insecure and gives them a unique love-hate relationship with Overseasia. They can't give it up. They are not sure it's good for them.

Just as New Zealanders insulate the economy, they protect their society with the Pohutukawa Curtain. They keep colourful scenes out of their films, colourful language out of their books, and colourful people out of their portals. Visitors come, but to the careful purdah of hotels no New Zealander can afford or military bases no New Zealander can visit. The Wellington diplomatic corps finds this the most stimulating country in the world. They meet only each other. News comes, like motorcars, in c.k.d. form so it can be assembled and pasteurised. The Indecent Publications Tribunal protects the people from perversion. Travel broadens only the overseas deficit so New Zealand has an elaborate system of exchange

161

control to ensure that as few as possible go overseas and that those who do go suffer the maximum inconvenience.

Yet protection is feeble. Overseasia pours in, filling the television screens and the papers. It provides the dynamics of change and uncertainty in a contented, conservative society. Skirts are tugged up and down by foreigners. Fashions are imported. Are American students revolting? Are politicians overseas talking about pollution? Large numbers of importers earn a living by copying overseas trends—from the hairdresser with the sign 'Fred of London', to the cover version of a hit record, or the cover version of see-through fashions. Naturally some fields respond more quickly than others. The police decide not to show an overseas film on crime prevention: it would teach the criminals tricks they'd not yet aspired to. Yet everywhere the time lags are getting shorter.

Smallness makes New Zealand provincial and incomplete. The able and ambitious go overseas where the top rungs of so many career ladders lie. The nation exports brains and imports brawn. It has sent a whole range of people overseas, from Rutherford to a pretender to the throne of Poland, whose scope for developing his potential in New Zealand was clearly limited. Some slip out the backdoor like John Rowles, others walk across the Tasman like Graham Kerr. New Zealand produces the best expatriates in the world. Overseasia sends back second-class brains and its faded talents. The pop stars of the past, from Millie Small and Dickie Valentine to Gene Pitney, were all last seen alive on tours of Australia or New Zealand.

Kiwis' reactions to their own expatriates are ambiguous. Revisiting Australia, Barry Humphries was asked by a television interviewer if he would stay. Answering 'No', he got the angry retort, 'What's the matter—aren't we good enough for you?' Next time he was faced with the same question a sense of public relations led him to say 'Yes'. 'Didn't you make it over there?' came the reply. Kiwis are the same. When their countrymen go and stay they're half resentful, half proud. If they go and come back, they're half relieved, half suspicious, doubting whether anyone faced with a choice

between money and New Zealand would choose New Zealand. If they don't go at all, it is assumed they're no good.

All this happens because New Zealand is small and unsure. Kiwis are happy, but there aren't that many of them and they may be wrong. Overseasia, therefore, confers approval. In the East they beg for alms from visitors. Kiwis bludge praise. Internationally they stand waiting for pats—for their race relations, butter, efforts in Vietnam or Pavlova cakes. The Governor-General is usually a Pom because only when an Englishman praises do Kiwis really believe it. Honours must appear to come from the Queen. It wouldn't do if the truth got out that knighthoods are rewards for making a lot of money, C.B.Es for less, and that all are decided by the Prime Minister.

Unfortunately, instead of patting, Overseasia ignores New

Zealand. Kiwis are proud of their achievements; no one knows what they are. In 1960 Mr Holyoake trotted overseas to 'see which countries were worthy of New Zealand's friendship' (*Freedom*, 9 February 1960). Few even knew where the country was. The Americans haven't troubled much about New Zealand because it hasn't yet shot any of their ambassadors or asked for arms to crush a communist rising at the Northland end of the domino pitch. The Australians take Kiwis for half-baked Poms; the British just take them for granted like the family pet. If they communicate at all it's to inquire the length of the harbour bridge connecting Auckland to Sydney. Overseasia fills the papers because there isn't much local news, but New Zealand news gets little overseas coverage—perhaps a couple of items a month in the qualities. The periodic replays of the warders versus inmates match at Mount Eden gets some attention, but it would take the submergence of the entire North Island to make the front page. Interest in the New Zealand welfare state is dead. Everywhere the Kiwi tourists' plaintive cry of, 'We're New Zealanders you know' is met by silence or, at best, a condescending, 'Oh you must know Bill Sourbutts from Adelaide'.

The indifference puts Kiwis at a loss. Half defiant, because they are proud of themselves, half uncertain because they're not sure how to behave. With the non-English world they wonder uneasily whether to refer to brown skins as Negro, coloured, black or non-Caucasian. They hide their embarrassment behind hearty condescension and pidgin English. Sir Keith admonished the Japanese to drink more milk and eat more meat to grow up big and strong, and presumably slow their economic growth rate down to New Zealand's. Sir Sidney Holland was observed to keep his hand over his wallet pocket when talking to Asian diplomats.

With the English and Continentals, New Zealanders feel rough and ready. English reactions are often suavely dismissive, as in this description of Sir Sidney Holland by a bemused British High Commissioner: '. . . at every dinner party, whether he was host or guest, he performed his conjuring tricks with the zest of an overgrown boy, delighting to remove your waistcoat without removing your coat and so forth. At our first meeting at dinner he illustrated his stupendous catch of an immense marlin in the Bay of Islands by using my wife as the fish and landing her on the sofa with many hugs and pats.'

Kiwi unease produces diverse reactions. Some practise curtsies for months before each royal visit. Though each visit is billed as less formal than the last, Prince Philip has yet to be seen at the piecart. Others take refuge in bravado, running the risk of being taken overseas for a financially embarrassed Australian. A few escape into silence with the less appalling risk of being taken for a deaf mute.

New Zealanders don't really understand an Overseasia that has changed since the old imperial days when one coat of red covered any colour. Kipling is alive and living in Remuera. War also distorted perspectives. Busloads of New Zealand tourists whistled the theme from *Bridge on the River Kwai* as their buses went through Tokyo to Expo 70. R.S.A. members stick to the original Auckland harbour bridge, refusing to use the Nippon clip-on. The Kiwi world is still divided into John Wayne's team versus the rest. Red Chinese imperialism, the

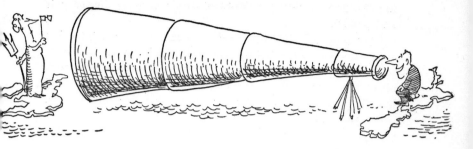

Orange Peril, poses almost as big a threat as foot and mouth.

This cruel world has little gratitude for what New Zealand has done for it. Three times it made the world fit for British cars to break down in, only to discover that the British will even sell us down the river for a common agricultural policy. Being L.B.J's poodle was hardly more satisfactory. True, New Zealand did get its instructions in person and the alliance did bring some of the world's finest minds from Spiro Agnew to Gang Aft Aglay, the Vietnamese chargé d'affaires in Petone, out to New Zealand for the occasional police benefit nights. Yet, however many men were sent to Vietnam it didn't help much with beef quotas or butter stocks.

A poodle without a master, a suburb without a city, a province without a capital—New Zealand's is the loneliness of the long-distance food supplier. The only resort is to advertise, 'Good, loyal limpet seeks firm rock'.

In despair many Kiwis have given up Overseasia, regarding it as a distant and annoying background noise, like the neighbours giving a party. Yet not all take this view. Though Kiwis are less and less sure where to find Mecca, every year more and more of them go overseas to look for it, while others take the poor man's escape ticket and drink themselves into frequent stupors.

Most go to Australia, a cut-price substitute for Overseasia, which bears the same relationship to it as a naughty weekend to marriage. Others go to America, over 20,000 a year. About the same number get through the minefields and barbed immigration officers into Britain, particularly if they're pale and patrial.

Four types of New Zealanders go to Overseasia. The first group go on business, wearing khaki uniforms in war, grey suits in peace. Businessmen try to combine work with pleasure, one reason for our increasing trade with Japan and Las Vegas. Politicians go to find facts, often in short supply. On 6 June 1969 the Minister of Defence returned announcing, 'I have received no indication from the Americans while I was in Vietnam that any more troops would be withdrawn this year.' Three days later the Americans pulled out 25,000. This does not invalidate fact finding. Mr Thomson had picked the wrong ones.

Next come the trippers. They pay for themselves. Eighteenth century England sent young nobles on the Grand Tour; twentieth century New Zealand prefers senior citizens. Farmers retire for it, public servants are rewarded with it, middle-aged men look forward to it—the Great Overseas Trip. Inconspicuous apart from their Air New Zealand bags and several hundredweight of fernleaf badges, they mingle with the natives. Unfortunately by Cook's Law, as countries get better to live in they are less attractive to visit, and Europe is well off. The history and tradition the trippers yearn for is phoney. The past is an adjunct of the automobile industry. Country vicars offer trading stamps to attract visitors: 'Take and stick this Green Stamp in remembrance that . . .' The Kiwi trippers tramp round and are duly disappointed.

New Zealand House exists to acquire and distribute Garden Party tickets (and the odds for getting one are one in three, or one in seven for Trooping the Colour) so they also participate in ceremonials, with equally disappointing results.

All the while they are wondering how the kids are getting on. Sir Keith summed up these home thoughts from abroad when he announced on one of his brief visits to New Zealand: 'I met the most important people abroad. I met their Majesties the King and Queen of Siam and President Kennedy of the U.S.A. But none has excited me as much as those four little New Zealanders, the Masons, in their cots.'

Most New Zealanders have similar feelings. They can't get home quick enough. The fact that Britain is a dirty dump, in the grip of pronounced moral decadence and equally pronounced black men helps reassure them that New Zealand is best. They can die happy. And broke.

The working holiday contingent are younger, mainly married couples and single girls. Men stay at home to acquire qualifications and sections. Girls go off to acquire culture and husbands. At first they cluster round New Zealand House, where the New Zealand skirt length going up meets the British coming down. Here they can feel at home, so friendly is the atmosphere, so bad the food. The green glass palace is the repository of all that's best in Britain. Small wonder that it is being mentioned in an increasing number of British guidebooks. The *Good Food Guide* it could never reach, but its lavatories have been praised in the *Good Loo Guide,* its girls are praised as the friendliest and easiest to pick up in the *Good Girl Guide,* hippies have brought it into their guides on free living as a good place to get a good sit-down and a read. Yet another guide suggests that those with time to kill should drop in on the free film shows.

While the hippies flood into New Zealand House the New Zealanders flood out as soon as they acclimatise. They continue to live with New Zealanders, which is the only reason they like London, but they revisit the womb occasionally and apologetically ('I only come because its got the best lavatories in London,' one told me).

Some visitors, festooned with cameras and meters, spend their time in Britain preserving on film a reality they're too busy to enjoy. Others follow up interests from culture to sex. Everything has to be crammed into a short stay so eat, drink and go to the Festival Hall. Tomorrow we return to New Zealand, to live on memories. A Kiwi removed from the constraints and social pressures of home is one without a conscience, and London offers life like they never had it in Waipukurau. Living twenty-four to a room in Earls Court, the Karangahape Road Extension, in conditions coloured immigrants would immediately report to the Race Relations Board, the trippers can afford those little luxuries—cinemas, laundrettes, tube trains, British rail sandwiches—that the natives can't. They enjoy it all to the full.

Others acclimatise. The Poms now view tradition in its true light as just another branch of British industry, differing only in that its plant is more rundown than the average. Many New Zealanders are, however, entranced by it. They also like English society, since they have the great advantage of being outside the class system. Indeed, by the purchase of thorn-proof suits and camel-hair coats they can rapidly acquire all its advantages without being programmed to its inhibitions. 'Funny thing the class system,' they murmur, recounting their weekend with Lord Fitz-Throwing. 'You know, they weren't at all snobbish. Treated us quite naturally.' Eagerly they follow up introductions to the peerage supplied in offhand moments by Governors-General or the Royal Commonwealth Society and eagerly stored in the list of contacts which every Kiwi carries. They descend on *Debrett* like house-trained Visigoths. Within a short time they become more English than the English. Soon they are lamenting New Zealand's egalitarianism, even the loss of India. When I was at Oxford it was always the Kiwis who fought to retain gowns, proctors, gate fines, sconces and all the other things which helped educate the élite of a technological society.

Perhaps all this is harmless. After all, Overseasia is a kind of finishing school for New Zealand. The problems really arise when the tripper gets back home. Some find that they

have to put the community conscience back on. It sits uneasily. Others become a kind of English fifth column, perpetually disgruntled, treating you, dear Keith, with blank hostility when you tell them you grew up in Britain and know its a dump. Most become My Trip Bores, re-living the experience in endless slide evenings; Messrs Kodak have a lot to answer for when the International Bore Crimes Tribunal convenes. Those girls who've not managed to secure a husband overseas return desperately predatory to a home where they are now too sophisticated and too old for a marriage market, or rather scrum, where every eligible male is snapped up at seventeen. Their slogan is the same as the Mounties'. They work in much the same way.

Before I forget them, I'd better tell you about the last lot of overseas visitors, the careerists. The New Zealander overseas has real advantages—all-round skills, ability to get on with people, honesty; and they aren't conditioned to know their place in the way the English are. They just climb the career ladder without wasting their time arguing over points of principle or politics. Yet are they New Zealanders? They feature in the New Zealand *Who's Who,* one-tenth of whose contents are overseas; it's certainly not a *Who's Here.* The press chronicles them as New Zealand born, as in the *Evening Post* headline on Dr Pickering: 'New Zealand's link with outer space'. They put in a ritual annual appearance at New Zealand House, particularly if they hope for an honour or a paid trip home as Governor-General. For them the clock stopped in New Zealand on the day they left. New Zealand thinks more of them than they of it. They are English in all but an accident of birth.

The careerists never come back unless to a retirement post of massive dignity and small functions. Yet they do share one thing with the trippers: they paint a depressing picture of New Zealand. Each year Kiwis spend an increasing total on overseas travel, a total many times higher than the expenditure on overseas representation. Public relations would dictate the reversal of these priorities. As fast as the overseas representatives can paint a rosy picture of home, the tourists smear it, talking loudly of the stew of mediocrity. The only solution is to keep them all at home. It's a pointless exercise to export the best brains and import second class—or, for manning the N.Z.B.C., third class—English ones. Come home Kiwi, all is forgiven. Then New Zealanders can build a nation together, using their skills instead of putting them at the free disposal of an ungrateful Edward Heath.

I would personally form a Society for the Abolition of Overseasia, for I doubt whether it's all worth the trouble. A few motorcars might grind to a halt for lack of spares. One thing, and only one, deters me. New Zealand may need Overseasia some day. After all, if the economic situation gets any worse, what with Common Market, food levies, butter gluts, beef quotas and the diminishing effectiveness of periodic doses of Muldoon medicine, then New Zealand will have to call in

Overseasia to rescue the nation from the Monetary and Economic Council.

How about a classified advertisement in the *International Exchange and Mart*: 'For Sale, Desirable Country, Almost New'. The Japanese might buy, for Toyko's overspill housing if their commuter trains get any faster, or perhaps the Kennedy family would be interested, as the last place where Teddy is going to be able to make a go of politics. The country might even get away without selling the freehold if it sent Tom Skinner and Hamilton Mitchell at the head of a posse of New Zealand mums to terrify the U.N. into giving some form of international outdoor relief. After all, New Zealanders have saved the world from enough perils. It's about time it did something for them.

Better still, next time the international committee on promotions and relegations meets New Zealand should write in the following terms:

Dear Sirs,
    I wish to apply for the position of Paraguay.
    My present position is New Zealand. In it I have rendered eminently satisfactory service, basing my behaviour on the best traditions of *Scouting for Boys* and performing many good deeds.
    George V, George VI and L. B. Johnson, my former pack leaders, are unfortunately now unable to provide testimonials. However, Mr Spiro Agnew is willing to testify on my behalf. I can also supply several glowing tributes from the *New Zealand Herald,* my auntie.
    I feel that I am now ready for the challenge of a bigger job with more scope. My present, very experienced government might get bored if its responsibilities are not enlarged. Mr Muldoon would, indeed, be willing to run New Zealand as well as Paraguay if this is any help to the new incumbent.

                                   Yours in anticipation,
                                   New Zealand

Such an application avoids any hint of desperation. There's no point in admitting that the alternative to removal is to sink beneath the waves.

The most desperate solution would be to export people. New Zealand now processes grass into animals. It could process the animals into people and export them. Countries with problems could then rent the entire Kiwi population. Previously New Zealanders have been called in only when the situation has been desperate. Afterwards they have come home to enjoy action replays at the R.S.A. Now they would go earlier. In Britain some could take over the car industry, produce better cars more cheaply and leave the British worker free to get on with the one thing he's really good at—striking.

Others would solve the housing by doing up the slums. Mums would take over factory and school canteens, ensuring that the British grew up healthy, fat and toothless. Some would encourage bathing, thus eliminating that B.O. fug which is forever England. They could make Britain a new country in nine months, France in two years. India might take a little longer. Then it would be back to New Zealand for a little holiday on the proceeds before putting in a bid for the U.S.A.

In this kind of future, Kiwis may need Overseasia. Now it's a curse. Perhaps they should boycott it. But seriously, until they do, I don't want to appear critical. The New Zealand trippers are the best in the world. Go to London and ask the English. They'll tell you so, provided you tip them.

PROCESSED POM

THE KIWIS. There they are. Love them or leave them. You can now decide whether to take out tenure or to renege on your assisted passage by pleading insanity. The plea will be accepted. The Kiwi tends to feel, with only sense, truth and justice to support the view, that no one in his right mind would go back to the dump you've just come from.

To be absolutely objective, there are reasons for leaving. It all depends on your own personal balance sheet of priorities. If you're a dedicated follower of fashion there's no point in staying. You'll be behind the rest of the world and no one will admire you or even notice if you set the pace. If you think excellence is within your capabilities, you're better off overseas with all the stimulus, the recognition and the acclaim. Remember, though, that one man's dynamic society is another's unemployment benefit.

If you're an ordinary mortal, stay. You can live life as it's meant to be lived: in a three bedroomed box with a beach not far away. You're free to choose your own destiny and rough hew it on a do-it-yourself basis. You can become a Polynesian amnesian, a business tycoon, pretender to the throne of Stewart Island, or take a lowly job as Director-General of the N.Z.B.C. No one will notice. No one will care. No one will hound you up the ladder, or kick you down again. It's all up to you.

As an immigrant, some doors are closed to you. Yet opportunity is wide open in anything which demands articulateness, extroversion, aggression or plain native cunning and duplicity. Small wonder that the Poms predominate in television. In the universities they are the most active section of the staff and the most profuse publishers. When I arrived I was taken to task by New Zealand academics for blundering into fields they regarded as theirs, though they had never bothered to fence, let alone till, them. Like the Negroes in the U.S.A., immigrants also rise through pop, show business and the native nicknackery industry. Even the nationalism industry has had immigrants, such as Professor Finlay, Peter Fraser, Walter Nash and W. B. Sutch, as its leaders. Small

wonder, because they're also among New Zealand's most active critics. The soprano section of the chorus of complaint is manned almost entirely by disgruntled immigrants, the kind of person who never buys a six pack of coke because he might be going home soon.

Unfortunately as an immigrant you can never sink into that happy quiescent norm of being a New Zealander. For the rest of your life you'll remain at best an apprentice. Even the immigrant teachers can beat them but never join them. The most simple-minded admiration of all things New Zealand from the Federation of Labour to N.Z.R. sandwiches will avail you naught. Your accent will always distinguish you: my northern burr was frequently taken for Dutch by old ladies who began to converse with me in pigeon English. You'll stand out because of your class complexes and your neuroses: on a beach of exposed brown flesh the only dirty thoughts will be inside *your* head. You'll be different because of your attitude to the outside world, and your frame of reference. Criticise and people will resent you, praise and they'll be suspicious, keep silent and they'll kick you. I vividly remember lecturing to a Tin Hat Club. I expressed my fervent admiration for the New Zealand constitution, my grovelling delight at her political parties. The audience relapsed into a drunken stupor, except one wizened Anzac who came up to me and hissed, 'You're not one of us'. *In Dominion Bitter Veritas.*

The consolation is that you're free to enjoy all that's best with a heightened perception. Years of crowded cities, rush-hour scrimmages, traffic pressures will turn you into an addict of open space and freedom. The conditioning of a class society where élites are creamed off and heavily rewarded while the skimmed milk is left to curdle will make you enthuse for an open society where no one is a social reject, no lot is permanent. Years of living in a land man has made ugly will show the advantages of a country where even the Ministry of Works and Comalco have only managed to scratch the surface. The pressures of a poor, polluted, troubled world will prepare you for the happiness of isolation.

Watch the sun setting on the Remarkables, sail down the Marlborough Sounds, swelter in the subtropical splendour of the Bay of Islands, or just lie on the beach or drive round the harbour—any beach and any harbour—and you know, even if no one else does, that this is as near to paradise as any non-Catholic nation is allowed to go. Even if you remove nature, the uniquely New Zealand aspects of life, things as eternal as skirt lengths in Hawke's Bay, are a multitude of minor pleasures. The peace of a double ration of Sundays,

the boozy camaraderie of a late afternoon's drinking, the quiet pleasure of a walk to the dairy for the Sunday papers, the crowded bustle of a Friday night shopping, the sleepy swelter of a summer beach—all yours. Enjoy them before the efficiency experts take them away or the rest of the world crowds in and swamps the place. If only we could stop the rush to change New Zealand.

Unfortunately, we can't. We have our problems: more and more of them and more and more pressing ones. The certainties have vanished; Albion is more perfidious than anyone had thought possible. New markets demand change, adjustment, new industries and an end to old certainties. The trinity of Wool Board, Meat Board and Dairy Board can no longer save the country. Hesitantly, reluctantly, the New Zealander is being forced to stand upon his own two knees. Yet even this is an excitement. There is a nation still to be built in New Zealand's green and pleasant land, an identity still to be forged. Together you're building a nation. And you couldn't have picked a better place for it.

I only wish I was there to give a hand. In this nasty, over-crowded and polluted world New Zealand is as near to a people's paradise as fallible humanity is likely to get.

Teach Yourself New Zild

AN AMERICAN ACCENT makes Kiwis cast anxious glances at their womenfolk, to make sure they're all safely talking to each other, but otherwise they like it, particularly if it conveys congratulations on how well they speak English. Being British, your lot is more difficult. Upper class accents produce defensive giggles, regional accents meet with the same blank stares as Japanese tourists. Only the Scots are accepted, though even their tones bring endless boring exchanges about ancestors in Kircudbright or offers of jobs in radio and television commercials for patent medicines or in the Dunedin Savings Bank.

Verbal communication is a luxury. This is a physical country and words neither do things nor mend cars. Words can even be dangerous and disruptive. They articulate emotions, express ideas, reveal personalities—activities New Zealanders have little taste for. So their children are brought up on the basic precepts that empty vessels make the most noise, particularly if they belong to the Union Steam Ship Company, and children should be seen and not heard. Students in school and college are conditioned to the view that knowledge is something to be doled out in carefully measured doses. The first aim in sexual relationships is to get married, so as to reduce the need to talk. In personal relationships, Kiwis relapse into mateship, communication by grunt.

Say nothing and smile vacantly. This establishes you as sound, reliable and sincere. If silence is impossible, beware of talking too much. This evokes distrust. Those who can't keep quiet are relegated to the low paid backwater of teaching or the high paid impotence of Parliament. The silent Public Service has the real power. If you must talk, far better to drag the words forth one by one, interspersing them with frequent 'I dunno—buts' and giving the impression that each word has been deep quarried from your soul and that the exercise leaves you exhausted.

Now you must understand New Zild as she is spoke. Elocution teachers sometimes say that New Zild is only lazy speech. They want to transform it into something akin to that finest product of elocutionary art, Sir Keith's rolling Kiwi Churchillianisms. In fact, New Zild is a substitute for speech, a verbal shorthand. New Zilders speak slowly as if they were boring themselves into sleep. They move lips as little as possible. The good New Zilder speaks like a ventriloquist without a dummy, so film editors often find it impossible to synchronise sound to lip non-movements and have been known to ignite themselves on a pyre of offcuts. New Zilders never use two syllables where one will do, either eliding sounds or contracting words. Their ideal is to run as many words as possible together to produce a continuous flow of diffident mumble. The race commentator would be the Kiwi Cicero if he weren't so strident.

Eventually the Linguistic Research Unit at Auckland will eliminate language altogether and replace it by a code of nods, winks and touches on the shoulder. Until then, the people communicate as much as possible by a sort of verbal stamp swapping of proverbs. Some of these, and some of the words used, will be unfamiliar to you. To help, here is a handy phrase book:

Anzac: In New Zealand a New Zealand soldier. In Australia an Australian soldier. In Britain an enzyme soap powder which is slightly less of a biological miracle than the other two.

'Are you there': Expression of incredulity that the telephone service, despite all its inefficiency, has allowed you to reach someone. Avoid any temptation to reply, 'Where the hell do you think I am'.

award rate: Pay no one actually gets. Discussions on wages and salaries concentrate on this so that no one is embarrassed by having his income revealed, and no one feels involved.

bach: Log cabin, evocative of where Johann Sebastian and Keith Jacka were born. Also known as a crib in Dunedin which copied the style.

backblocks: Remote country, named after the tackle needed to repair the car after you've driven there.

Benghazi burner: A little known weapon of war. Left burning by the roadside it would either explode in the face of German troops or poison them with a rust coloured liquid.

bomb: Strategic nuclear device on wheels.

borer: Explanation of your inability to get a long mortgage.

cockie: Farmer who turns mud into milk.

closed party: Party with fewer than five gatecrashers per invitee.

crook: State of health after eating local food.

cut: Drunk.

dash: Mild expletive uttered when lemonade is found in beer.

fair dinkum: Blond Australian.

favourite: State of happiness, known often to horses.

'a few beers': 'I met Joe and we had a few beers' means probably that they drank solidly from Friday night to Sunday.

glory box: Bottom drawer with lid on. View with alarm any girl who talks about hers. Some girls have glory boxes so big they live in them.

haka: Concession to race relations by N.Z. Rugby Union.

half-G: Less than 50 per cent of a full-G. Also known in Dunedin as a peter, after the first missionary to land in that city, St Peter Speight.

Hokonui: Import substitute Scotch.

hooray: Lamentation and expression of regret at being parted from someone, e.g., 'I must go now. Hooray.'

joker: Surly, sullen individual; average Kiwi.

Judy: Naughty sister of Sheila.

larrikin: Young people of whom you happen not to approve. Note that all the terms of disapprobation for rumbustious youth left the rest of the world when youth took it over and crawled off to die in New Zealand where the old have such a strong hold. Expressions still used are 'milk-bar cowboy', 'flagon wagon gang' and even occasionally 'Teddy boy'.

Manchester: Japanese cotton goods. One proud Lancashire lass who told a Dunedin shop assistant, 'I come from Manchester', was answered, 'Yes, there are a lot of people up from the country today'.

Nats: Government of New Zealand from time immemorial.

paua shell: Product of West German jewellery industry.

Pom: Suspected Englishman. The confirmed case is referred to in the clinical term of Pongo.

poufter: Air mattress assembler or M.P.

pozzie: Position.

Rafferty's rules: Standing Orders of the House of Representatives. Named after William Ewart Rafferty, the second Speaker who, because of his high voice, was also referred to as Mr Squeaker.

ratbag: Bag of rats, or M.P.

red fed: Non-member of National Party.

remit: Resolution.

remittance man: Immigrant assisted from the other end. A nineteenth century aristocracy whose pre-eminence is now usurped by the non-remittance man.

Sheila: Female New Zealander. On marriage she changes her name to 'the wife'.

'She'll be right': An expression of faith in divine providence.

sparrow fart: Time so early in the morning no English immigrant has ever heard this mysterious noise. All New Zealanders hear it; indeed the sound of their housework probably disturbs the sparrow in the first place.

spot: Short drink.

T.A.B.: System of investment similar to purchase of shares in Mineral Securities or Rolls-Royce.

tailor made: Smokable cigarette. Sign of effeminacy. 'Roll your own' smokers can be seen in any graveyard. Keep a suspicious eye on rollers at your party—it could be pot. If it is, the effects will be far nicer than the roaring drunks around but the police won't like it. Bottle parties O.K. Pot parties illegal.

varsity: University where *Salad Days* has been performed. Much of the language and folklore of Edwardian Oxford survives in New Zealand.

the wog: Don't be alarmed if your girl friend is in bed with the wog. She has a virus infection known clinically as 'the bot'.

wowser: Anti-drink fanatic. Not to be confused with bowser, a man of spirit.

'You're not too foul': Highest compliment a man can pay to a woman. Avoid it as it could be a proposal of marriage. Next highest, 'You're a good bloke', is safer.

Please note. This brief vocabulary does not include the following words: ****, ****, ****, ****-***, ****, or ********. While much used in private conversation, in public they are germane only to the revolutionary branch of show biz and might give offence to police, rugby players and wharfies.

PRINTED BY WHITCOMBE AND TOMBS LIMITED
G5590